THE LOST ART OF DISCERNMENT

*America's Inability to Know
Right from Wrong*

ROLAND A. GUERRERO

Archway Publishing books may be ordered through booksellers or by contacting:

Archway Publishing
1663 Liberty Drive
Bloomington, IN 47403
www.archwaypublishing.com
844-669-3957

Because of the dynamic nature of the Internet, any web addresses or links contained in this book may have changed since publication and may no longer be valid. The views expressed in this work are solely those of the author and do not necessarily reflect the views of the publisher, and the publisher hereby disclaims any responsibility for them.

Any people depicted in stock imagery provided by Getty Images are models, and such images are being used for illustrative purposes only. Certain stock imagery © Getty Images.

Scripture texts in this work are taken from the *New American Bible*, revised edition© 2010, 1991, 1986, 1970 Confraternity of Christian Doctrine, Washington, D.C. and are used by permission of the copyright owner. All Rights Reserved. No part of the New American Bible may be reproduced in any form without permission in writing from the copyright owner.

ISBN: 978-1-6657-0731-2 (sc)
ISBN: 978-1-6657-0730-5 (hc)
ISBN: 978-1-6657-0732-9 (e)

Library of Congress Control Number: 2021910330

Printed in the United States of America.

Archway Publishing rev. date: 10/18/2021

This book is dedicated to St. Thomas More, to Dietrich Bonhoeffer, and to Congressman John Lewis. The cross of conscience leads to Easter light in a dark world.

CONTENTS

Preface ix

Introduction xi

THE PROCESS

Chapter 1   Smoke and Mirrors 1

Chapter 2   Words Matter 6

Chapter 3   The Premised Land 16

Chapter 4   A Smattering of Perspective 25

THE ISSUES

Chapter 5   The Flag 35

Chapter 6   Black Lives Matter 42

Chapter 7   Pro-Life, Pro-Choice, Pro-Fear, and Accusation 60

Chapter 8   A Chicken in Every Pot and a Gun in
            Every Hand 73

Chapter 9   The Death of Reason: The Either/Or Trap
            and Other False Dichotomies 84

Chapter 10 The Politics of Sexuality 107

Chapter 11 The Separation of Church and State and
            Swallowing a Camel 128

Chapter 12 The Emperor Is Butt Naked: The Trump
            Problem, the Us Problem 147

Chapter 13 The Millstone and the Trap:
            An Epistle to Christians 157

Postscript July 30, 2020 169

PREFACE

The writing of this book began on the Ash Wednesday morning of February 14, 2018, which of course also happened to be Valentine's Day and most notoriously was the day that the students and faculty of Marjory Stoneman Douglas High School were terrorized by the murderer of seventeen people later that afternoon. I had put off the writing of this book countless times but felt inspired to use the start date of Ash Wednesday and the focus of a Lenten discipline to finally quit making excuses, such as "Who am I?" and "Who really cares?" as if those things mattered at all. I was busting at the seams and could no longer resist the deluge of pressure building up inside me.

As the manuscript was well on the way to completion, there was a massacre on August 3, 2019, at a Walmart in my hometown of El Paso, Texas. The shock and disbelief that accompany the expression "Not in my town" remain nearly eight months later.

As I write this preface, it is March 31, 2020, and to date, yesterday was the recording of the greatest single day total of deaths in the US due to COVID-19 at 500, and the national death toll was around 3,100. We have not been so divided as a nation since the Civil War itself yet have such a rare opportunity to overcome our divisions as we face a common threat.

Such were the times in which this book was written.

INTRODUCTION

One might ask, "What is discernment anyway?" and could be forgiven for not having the answer on the tip of the tongue. Just as we have moved away from appearing to moralize out of the fear of imposing our ethical views onto someone else, we have also abandoned the most basic discipline of critical thinking in both the interior life as well as in one's interaction with the world. Because popular opinion has become exceedingly polarized or "tribalized" on a single dimension, it is no surprise that we find ourselves increasingly alienated from "the other." Discernment about who I am and about my relation to humanity can help us discover that the "other" is just a construct, but one that is very difficult to lobotomize from our consciousness.

In Christianity, the word *discernment* may have several meanings. It can be used to describe the process of determining God's desire in a situation or for one's life or identifying the true nature of a thing, such as discerning whether a thing is good or evil. In large part, it describes the interior search for an answer to the question of one's vocation, namely determining whether God is calling one to the married life, single life, consecrated life, ordained ministry, or any other calling.

Now with the introduction of all these concepts, there is just one more to address in this age of echo chamber realities given life by participation in online communities. The Greek word is *kritikos,* which means to be able to judge or discern.

One might add that kritikos is simply the ability to distinguish right from wrong and good from bad. Even though our English usage of the words *critical* and *criticize* carries some very negative connotations, this is not always the case.

Some of my most treasured memories of performing as a musician in school for my peers was the opportunity to be critiqued by others. Since I had a great desire to improve my musicianship and overall performance level, the critiques were always a source of information and perspective that, because of my own subjective blinders, I could not perceive on my own. This point is *critical* in that a prerequisite for desiring to know any truth of any kind is humility, particularly when it comes to improving oneself and freely admitting and addressing one's own limitations.

A Christian would also have to consider this passage from Romans:

> I urge you therefore, brothers, by the mercies of God, to offer your bodies as a living sacrifice, holy and pleasing to God, your spiritual worship.
>
> Do not conform yourselves to this age but be transformed by the renewal of your mind, that you may discern what is the will of God, what is good and pleasing and perfect. (Romans 12:1–2 NAB)

This passage comes closest to what discernment means to me, and the following concepts will occur throughout the following chapters:

1. Humility. Know the truth about yourself, your strengths, your weaknesses, your talents, your limitations, and so

on. Don't deceive yourself. Let go of the illusion of being right. Saul had to believe he was right. Paul learned to walk the path of humility.

2. Openness. Have an open mind and an open heart so that ongoing transformation becomes a way of life. Be open to the pain of encountering others on a common journey.

3. Kritikos. Develop a healthy critical consciousness. Avoid groupthink and tribalism. Judge with honest clarity your motives and perceptions, but avoid judging others. Learn to listen to your conscience as you begin to know yourself.

4. Compassion. Know that discernment is not a process made in a private lab in a test tube within a vacuum. It is always about relationship and response. It draws on one's personal history within a culture and family and expands to connectedness to all creation—that which is holy. Allow the needs of others to inform your discernment.

SECTION ①

THE PROCESS

ONE

SMOKE AND MIRRORS

Who controls the past controls the future. Who
controls the present controls the past. War is
peace. Freedom is slavery. Ignorance is strength.

GEORGE ORWELL

It has occurred to me on and off the last few decades that if the effects and outcomes depicted in *1984* really did occur in 1984, then we would be oblivious to the fact that anything happened at all. The only evidence is that not only would people be spoon-fed today's flavor of reality but they would be incapable of seeing contradiction or inconsistency and wouldn't even care if the "truth" was a lie. Wait a minute. Maybe it did really happen.

So what is reality in this day of "reality" shows and conspiracy theories? As a statement attributed to Mark Twain indicates, why is it that "a lie can travel halfway around the world while the truth is putting on its shoes"? And more importantly, why are we so predisposed to believe lies? When did caring for the truth stop mattering to so many people? Secondly, who do you *really* trust anymore? What people and/or institutions did you used to place trust in but no longer do? Is trust for you relational or ideological, earned or freely given, or societal or tribal? What do you do when trust and deception become partners and you can't separate where one starts and the other ends?

Back in the days when Walter Cronkite was considered the most trusted man in America, journalism and journalists were respected not only as a source of the truth but as essential components to a free and democratic society. How did our compass for gauging the truth, hand in hand with a trusting spirit, devolve into the www.misinformation nightmare we have allowed ourselves to slavishly consult as to what our opinions should be today? When did we surrender our brain cells for ideological frontal lobotomies?

Perhaps trust was the first casualty in the abandonment of truth. For those old enough to remember, how was your sense of trust and stability affected by the assassinations of the sixties or the civil rights movement, the Kent State massacre, the Pentagon Papers, or the Watergate scandal? How well did your psyche survive the Vietnam War, regardless of if you supported it or not? Even our religious affiliation can be an invitation to lose trust as parents and church leaders inevitably fail to live up to what is professed or, more realistically, to our perceptions of how they should act. Human failings often provide us with the reasons to lose trust at the expense of learning compassion and forgiveness. Traumatic experiences as a result of abuse by those we thought we could trust have long-lasting effects where all bets are off regarding handing one's trust to any person, any institution, or any symbol of authority.

Lastly, what role do both fearfulness and fearmongering have in switching off the intellect and at the same time reinforcing tribal instincts and self-preservation engrams to create "truths" so as to believe the worst about other people? How has the inability to trust anyone outside one's tribe allowed for the manipulation of tribal fears, which don't necessarily have any basis in reality?

If all these issues weren't enough, how does one discern what is true when all manner of outrageous claims are made for products aimed at our insecurities regarding weight loss, sexual potency, body odor, beauty aids, and a host of other conditions, all without a sliver of scientific data to back them up? Pseudoscience, built on ad campaigns dramatizing experts in white lab coats and testimonials by "real" people, also contribute to the confusion regarding topics ranging from the search for whiter teeth to the ultimate cures for arthritis and back pain. To make matters worse, there seems to be a five-year cycle of "credible" studies promoting and then alternately dismissing the inherent value of a glass of wine a day, butter, aspirin, vitamin C, vitamins, or any dairy products at all, not to mention eggs.

How many times have you parroted these "findings" to other people without doing one iota of research yourself to verify the authenticity of the study, a process akin to gossip? Who financed the study? What method of testing was used? Was there a peer review of the study? Why don't news outlets do this research before they disseminate what could be completely false information?

Information gathering is a critical part of discernment. I remember from my minor seminary days the term "affected ignorance." This entails suspecting that my actions may be morally sinful, but I'm not absolutely certain and I deliberately choose not to research and inform myself because I may not like what I find. The individual is choosing to reinforce his or her purpose, or "truth," by remaining ignorant. People would often rather not shed any light at all on the subject. The function of affected ignorance is to buttress up one's rationalizations or, in simpler terms, to cut oneself some slack and get away with it. This slack allows the individual to maintain a spurious foundation of justification and to hold on to a false belief system that insulates a malformed conscience. Wrong becomes right.

When we apply this understanding to how gullible we can allow ourselves to be, we might notice a lack of due diligence in even attempting to get all the facts on a study, a rumor, or a political position. Swallowing misinformation hook, line, and sinker reflects the opposite of a discerning heart, but there are motives for remaining ignorant. Antivaxxers really believe they are protecting their children even though there are mountains of evidence to the contrary. The critical point is that other children are put at risk and can become ill or even die as a result of epidemics that can be prevented. Antivaxxer misinformation/propaganda is very slick and very untrue, but people fall for it every day.

The motives behind antigovernment groups are also worth examining. Timothy McVeigh's blind righteousness led to the deaths of 168 people with almost seven hundred others injured in Oklahoma City. Individual ignorance combined with self-righteousness disregards the collective needs and rights of the community so much so that the ideological "cause" is held in greater esteem than real people. Antigovernment sentiments can be found throughout the internet, but they are fundamentally different from governmental watchdog groups, whistleblower concerns, and websites dedicated to governmental overreach.

Most would agree that it would be naive to blindly trust the government in all things at all times, but discerning between groups that want accountability and oversight and groups that are simply antigovernment is not that difficult. The former usually believe in America and want to be part of the solution for when the country does not live up to its ideals. Think of "a more perfect union." The latter usually has an axe to grind and both projects and appeals to a great deal of raw, negative emotions. Not unlike the white nationalist movement, most of those attracted to antigovernment websites are very angry White males who share a sense of being disenfranchised somehow. This is a form of tribal identification.

Critical thinking casts light while skepticism casts doubt. Without having to completely dissect the motives of McVeigh and his ilk or of antivaxxers or of conspiracy theorists in general, a sincere discernment by an individual would have to first observe that the three common denominators of casting doubt, creating mistrust, and instilling fear are central to the message of these groups. True critical thinking is abandoned where reason is replaced by extreme emotion and enabled with convoluted logic. The underlying sophistries employed are thrown together for the sole purpose of promoting agendas and not for the seeking of truth. This same process occurs in political campaigns, commercial ads, and cable pseudonews networks.

The second, and almost more important, issue is for the discerning individual to observe if the message and the emotions behind it are in fact appealing and relatable. Does one identify with the message or group? This can be very tricky because deception takes root where self-deception has already tilled the soil.

TWO

WORDS MATTER

He summoned the crowd and said to them, "Hear
and understand. It is not what enters one's mouth that
defiles that person; but what comes out of the mouth
is what defiles one." Then his disciples approached
and said to him, "Do you know that the Pharisees
took offense when they heard what you said?"

MATTHEW 15:10–12 (NAB)

This is such a great reading from the gospel of Matthew as it not only refers to the destructive motives behind poisonous words but it also refers to taking offense to words as the Pharisees did. As we perceive each other's words through the filter of our biases, we either form connections with others or create division. Do I carefully listen when another speaks, or am I too busy formulating a rebuttal? As we use words either thoughtfully or with disregard for how others perceive them, we communicate acceptance or rejection of the "other." Sometimes we communicate indifference.

The potential of words being relational for us or increasing antagonism between us or, even worse, being dismissive altogether is enough reason to explore the moral implications of our speech and the formation of conscience, which is either enhanced or suppressed in the process. This same formation of conscience must also deal directly with one's defensiveness when confronted with opposing views. The more one's identity is enmeshed in one's worldview, the less capable the individual is of truly listening to others, with the end result being defensiveness.

Americans have a special place in their hearts for the First Amendment and the concept of free speech as an ideal, yet I propose that our perceived rights are not absolute and that our overriding concern for the concept of free speech has more to do with our affiliations and personal interests being served than for an objective respect for the Constitution of the United States of America. Even though there already exist extreme examples regarding the limitations of free speech in our country, such as not being able to shout, "Fire!" in a crowded theater, a genuine process of discernment leads me to examine not only my right to express myself but whether or not I should say whatever I choose without regard for others. Though freedom of speech and expression are very much a part of the American fabric, I would hardly place the same level of importance upon pornography or the use of foul language in a comic routine or music entertainment as I would on the freedom of the press or the right of a minority voice to be heard. The hypocrisy of foul language allows for it to flow unimpeded from Trump's mouth and unimpeded from many of Trump's detractors' mouths as they use coarse language to condemn each other's use of coarse language.

My identity as a Catholic Christian must inform my concept of personal rights against the backdrop of social responsibility in the formation of my conscience. As an American, I must also be guided by the "Preamble" to the United States Constitution so as to understand the purpose and guiding principles of the

Constitution as well as to use it as a basis for understanding the intentions of the Founding Fathers.

> We the People of the United States, in Order to form a more perfect Union, establish Justice, insure domestic Tranquility, provide for the common defence, promote the general Welfare, and secure the Blessings of Liberty to ourselves and our Posterity, do ordain and establish this Constitution for the United States of America.

If words really do matter, then I must fully appreciate the words "We the People," "form a more perfect Union," "common defense," "general welfare," and "to ourselves and our posterity." No matter how entrenched anyone is in the polarized world of conservatives against liberals regarding the constitutional rights of the individual, it would seem that a discerned reading of the "Preamble" would indicate that the language of the collective needs of the people is not by accident. Any objective constitutional position would almost have to be steeped in the language of the "Preamble" as it establishes a premise or intellectual precedent on how to read the Constitution.

Now to cut to the chase, I must lay bare my intentions for writing this book as I have no particular credentials to speak of. I am an expert at nothing. I am not even a very competent or persuasive writer for that matter. I discuss intentions because an accurate representation of one's true intent is what adds flesh to the bones of one's words. My intentions are simply to provide a means by which people may develop their own consciences regarding our present ideological impasses, both socially and politically, and may develop a deeper appreciation for their fellow Americans who think differently from themselves yet still draw from the same well that gives us a common American identity. Appreciating what we have in common can give us the tools for real dialogue and not merely the posturing of the two political parties. I am attempting to respond to how God is leading me as part of the gift of discernment I have been given to share and to draw others into their own serious discernment process. Although I would like as many people as possible to engage in this process of discernment involving critical consciousness, I also have a target audience of those people who claim to be Christian yet have allowed themselves to be taken up in waves of anger and hatred.

The ideals which we share can help us to appreciate the anger and frustration of those who find themselves confounded at every turn in dealing with bureaucracy, corporate greed, and ideological sacred cows, which end up hurting our fellow Americans. In the later chapters of this book, we will explore alternative ways of thinking by going beyond the single dimension of left and right linear roadblocks and adding the second dimension of common needs, which always demands a response and the third dimension of shared roots, wisdom, and vision. The words and understanding of these two other dimensions do not and cannot allow for any condemnation or oppression of the "other." Passing from the one-dimensional prison of polarized thinking to two- and three-dimensional awareness is akin to being beamed back onto the *Enterprise* where the "biofilters" eliminate contagions of hate from infecting one's view of others. This is so much more than thinking outside the box. It is a realization that the box needs to be discarded altogether as it is only a by-product of smoke and mirrors. From the perspective of the Catholic, I must ask myself, "What am I willing to die to?" so that others may live.

In spite of the inherent idealism such a process would require, what is an American if not an idealist? A good dose of common sense and street smarts is also required. Some groups or individuals differ only in perspective while others feed on divisiveness and fear. Those belonging to the latter will be incapable of such a process and can be identified by their—wait for it—words. Words intended to sow fear are a dead giveaway. Millions of advertising dollars go into fear-based marketing since it is a proven tool for manipulating the populace. Words that go way beyond merely casting doubt and are intended to create mistrust of others are also red flags. Use of the term "fake news" is a prime example of the rhetoric of mistrust. Yes, some information is patently false and intended to deceive and divide, but can I discern the difference between solid journalism and misinformation, and do I want to know the difference if it means that I have to take a critical look at my own bias filters?

Before the individual can begin to appreciate the full effects of the manipulation of fear and trust as it is practiced on cable news networks, online, and in politics, objective discernment demands that the microscope be turned onto oneself. Our own biases make us more susceptible to key buzzwords that can trigger both a fear response and paranoid suspicion.

Before one can turn the eyes of critical consciousness onto one's reality, those same eyes must be focused on one's own fear and trust issues. The process of individuals entering this kind of discernment is the lynchpin for the whole social dynamic because it can serve to inoculate the thinking process from susceptibility to manipulation due to unresolved personal baggage.

There can be no true dialogue with others who represent conflicting perspectives from us, unless all parties begin from a place of mutual respect and not from fear and from faith in shared ideals and not from mistrust. No amount of empirical data can counter conclusions drawn in fear. No amount of objective reasoning is sufficient to breach the wall of suspicion.

The primary function of promoting fear and mistrust is the closing of minds to "the other." Vladimir Putin has found this Achilles' heel to American democracy, which has its roots in the self-inflicted wound of tolerating negative campaign ads as the norm and not as something that is unacceptable in a civil society. The way to neutralize the threat of anyone who would wish to divide us is the concerted effort of people of good will to engage in civil discourse based on common goals where the "general welfare" is the overriding concern as opposed to the myopic attainment of self-interests or party interests.

With our words, we often begin the poisonous process of demonizing all who would dare hold an opposing opinion from ours and then make sweeping generalizations to attack the integrity of the opponent. Here are some examples of such words from the last fifty years with the relevant question being whether or not you relate to or sympathize with the divisive language:

> Police become pigs. Immigrants become rapists and murderers or people from "shit-hole" countries. Soldiers become baby killers. Pro-life advocates become kooks and religious fanatics. Pro-choice advocates become murderers. The press becomes fake news. Traditional marriage supporters become homophobes. Protesters taking a knee during the national anthem become unpatriotic "sons of bitches." Second Amendment advocates become gun fanatics. Gun control advocates become attackers of freedom. Black Lives Matter protestors become agitators and cop killers. Middle Eastern-looking people (whatever that means) become threats to national security. Political supporters of the

opposition become a "basket of deplorables." The political opponent becomes a "nasty woman."

I would invite the reader to identify any and all such demonizing tactics that you have encountered, that have targeted you, or that you have used against others. The reality is that by our deliberate choosing of words, we are either part of the problem or part of the solution. Silence automatically falls into the part of the problem column.

The coarseness of language and lack of respect for others that have become both the societal and online norm are justified by many as a response to the perception of overbearing political correctness in our society. This, coupled with an extreme reaction to the concept of censorship as it affects free speech issues, has created a hostile environment for civil discourse. Though part of the American mythos regards those people who shoot from the hip as plainspoken and matter-of-fact in character, oftentimes the exact opposite is the case where lies and misinformation are not discerned by a gullible audience who are more enthralled by the delivery than by the substance of what is being said. The reality is that a lie remains a lie no matter how many times it is repeated and no matter how many gullible people are taken in by snake oil men. The new application of Marshall McLuhan's famous phrase "The media is the message" seems to be "The messenger is the message." The more bombastic and crass the verbal gladiator is in the arena, the louder the crowd shouts for slaughter and blood. The basest instincts and vulgarest aspects of human nature will create and give homage to the gladiator in every arena possible, most notably the internet, Twitter, late-night television, and rubber-stamped "news" networks.

Nobody enjoys walking on eggshells as "PC" Nazis in the workplace play a power game where the free exchange of ideas is thwarted on behalf of the thin-skinned and the psychologically damaged. This mind-gamey manipulation of others is both toxic and counterproductive. I remember one job I had where I was expected to apologize to a fellow employee for something I said in a meeting because personal offense was taken. I used the term "everybody and their dog" and a person at the meeting thought that I was deliberately calling them a dog. They took my use of an expression personally. The situation had to be explained to me because I didn't have a clue as to how my use of a common phrase could get so twisted around and how someone could make the judgment of me that I would deliberately do such a thing. I was floored.

Some people on the "progressive" side of the PC game come up with what I consider absurd language such as the word Latinx. The linguistic attempt to practice inclusivity just alienates me to no end. I don't need somebody else's version of reality shoved down my throat, thank you. The right-wingers, those who supposedly despise any PC censoring at all in public discourse, have no problems linking any critique of Israel and Israeli influence in American politics with being anti-Semitic somehow. I suppose that Benjamin Gantz and all supporters of the Blue and Whites in Israel are Jewish anti-Semites.

The pendulum has most definitely swung the other way as the battle cries of those who long to throw off the chains of "PC" are nothing more than what the generations before the concept of political correctness even existed would have called rude and offensive. From local school board meetings to presidential campaigns, one can experience the full gamut of behavior that none of us would want our children to emulate. Real Nazis and hooded cowards have been given carte blanche in the current political climate to say what they have long held back in their nativist and nationalist camouflage. If it goose-steps like a racist and *talks* like a racist ... On the other end of the spectrum, you have the antifa fanatics who have, in their typically violent and ironically fascist-styled fashion, continued to impose their self-appointed role of arbiters of thought and speech on the rest of us. These are the two extremes, so to which are you closer according to our narrow left/right single dimension?

When one chooses to use the language of common needs, even recognizing that one needs those in opposition to oneself to get a clearer perspective of what is real, then those with differing points of view are no longer the "them" as defined by the tribal "us." This is the point at which second-dimensional possibilities of human interaction create ever new variations at finding solutions and leave behind imperatives, such as finding blame and casting doubt.

The unspoken language of this second dimension is service and can best be exemplified by the communal response to the most terrible of circumstances. The unselfish actions of first responders on 9/11 and in any town USA before and since gives us a taste of what this plane feels like. Not since the JFK assassination or the *Challenger* disaster had so many of us shared such a common plane of human emotion to the extreme or such a sense of national unity and purpose. No matter where you were from, the sense of what we held in common was palpable down to the "where were you when" conversations that helped us to accept the unacceptable. With every disaster since, where fellow Americans lose "everything," so to speak, there are those among us who rise to the occasion and give beyond human capacity because it is the right thing to do. This is a core characteristic of discernment. The choice to act, to serve, is so clear that it drowns out the doubts and objections cast by our one-dimensional trappings.

Please do not think that what is being proposed is merely a casting call for a Coca-Cola commercial where people are holding hands and singing "Kumbaya" or "It's the Real Thing." The very real and very painful journey of casting out one's demons in order to appreciate the unity of our common woundedness is not for the faint of heart. Should we and can we forgive ourselves? There is a great deal of self-forgiveness that needs to precede the ability to look at others with compassion. Compassion is such a great word—to suffer with. Also don't make the mistake of thinking that going beyond one-dimensional false dichotomies is a matter of spiritual or intellectual ascendency. On the contrary, all that is necessary is humility.

Later in the book, we will examine many if not all the hot button issues we have allowed to define and divide us. This examination is not meant to be exhaustive in the least but to only serve as a catalyst for further expansion by groups of people across the nation and possibly throughout the world. The challenge is becoming aware of commonalities between myself and people whose worldviews are entirely different and then valuing the reality that many of the commonalities are in fact core to being human and many of the differences are vestiges of cultural or ideological bias which serve no positive purpose. Discernment is the process of discovering the difference. After the examination of the issue at hand, each chapter will segue into a section called "Premise and Perspective," where I attempt to lay out for the reader my attempts at confronting the experiences in my life that have formed my biases and how I consciously integrate or discard well-developed concepts in my process of humbly admitting that my opinions are not sacred; they are just perspectives.

A question for the reader is whether you more often use words of divisiveness and anger in your encounters and online posts or words of encouragement and unity. Sometimes, the words one chooses to believe in and chooses to share with others are both the result and the reflection of who a person is becoming.

THREE

THE PREMISED LAND

Then God said: Let us make human beings in
our image, after our likeness. Let them have
dominion over the fish of the sea, the birds of
the air, the tame animals, all the wild animals,
and all the creatures that crawl on the earth.
God created mankind in his image; in
the image of God he created them;
male and female he created them.
God blessed them and God said to them: Be fertile
and multiply; fill the earth and subdue it. Have
dominion over the fish of the sea, the birds of the air,
and all the living things that crawl on the earth. God
also said: See, I give you every seed-bearing plant on
all the earth and every tree that has seed-bearing fruit
on it to be your food; and to all the wild animals, all
the birds of the air, and all the living creatures that
crawl on the earth, I give all the green plants for food.

GENESIS 1:26–30 (NAB)

The LORD God then took the man and settled him
in the garden of Eden, to cultivate and care for it.

GENESIS 2:15 (NAB)

So do I ultimately believe that I am the master of creation and that it is my God-given responsibility to subdue the natural world, or do I believe that I have the responsibility to be a benevolent steward of nature so as to maintain a balance, a harmonious relationship with the natural world? Belief in God is not even required to fall into one camp or the other. All the subterfuge surrounding business rights, ecology, gun rights, animal rights, medical ethics, energy consumption, manifest destiny, racism, etc. are mere surrogates for the creation premise upon which I form my opinions either consciously or not from the creation stories in Genesis. This can be true even if I consider the creation stories as pure myth.

A fundamental question that cannot be overlooked or considered a forgone conclusion is whether or not I am aware of the already existing premises upon which my opinions are based. In this day of predigested arguments, do I really understand the foundational thinking upon which both my reasoning and biases are built and in some cases even my construct of an identity upon which a sense of self is dependent? Am I so enmeshed in "identity politics" that I can't see beyond the interests of my tribe, even if the whole is ultimately damaged? It is also possible that I have adopted someone else's opinions and issues and that I am completely ignorant upon what premise "my" position is based. From such ignorance arises the possibility that I might find the relevant premises repugnant with further study.

History has the greatest value for us if we would but learn from it. Long before the sexual revolution of the sixties, the mores of the Victorian age, or the societal interdictions of the Puritans, there existed the tension between the hedonists and the Stoics. The Gnostics were very influential in a time when Rome was rife with all manner of orgies. To which among the many isms throughout history have I built an unconscious altar upon which I sacrifice my free will under the illusion of independent thought?

This is a simple retracing of my personal isms that have pulled my strings, so to speak. Hedonism begets objectivism begets capitalism begets consumerism begets the illusion of freedom of choice for products that I didn't know that I needed to be happy until I was convinced through clever marketing that my current happiness was insufficient and that I was in danger of losing whatever happiness I had unless I purchased what I obviously lacked. I have found that insomnia and wee hour infomercials are a very dangerous mix. Such is the legacy of one who was a child in the 1960s when the marriage of Saturday morning cartoons and the toy merchandising industry developed into a renaissance of mindless consumerism.

We can laugh at this all too prevalent scenario which by its commonality only adds to the humor, but this common experience would be completely lost on a family of subsistence farmers and gatherers from a third world country. Hopefully, this cultural disconnect might be enough of a motivation to first question and then change my way of thinking and being. The most hands-on discernment required is an open and honest reflection upon my wants versus my needs. The next discernment would be an intensive examination upon my emotional and psychological state as to why I am so easily manipulated by marketing strategies that aim at undermining my self-esteem. These steps would naturally lead to questions of lifestyle, career, values, and so on. All these steps are valuable in and of themselves but sometimes can only scratch the surface of the underlying mindset that functions as a premise to my bizarre, unconscious behavior. The fact is my less evolved self really buys into hedonism as a guilt-free way of living, which functions to anesthetize my sense of unhappiness.

I have outlined one tendril of personal ism progression that I have bought into and that I have subsequently come to reject in its entirety. In order to attempt to reject fundamental ways of thinking, which I no longer want to be influenced by, I need to focus on what is life-giving for me and for others. The hedonic treadmill, which guarantees that my sense of "happiness" will level off no matter how much stuff I amass, is a contemporary cycle of addiction that has me hypnotized by just the right infomercial. These modern behavioral addictions are nothing more than expressions of concupiscence for the twenty-first century. Romans 7:15 says, "What I do, I do not understand. For I do not do what I want, but I do what I hate."

Because my faith provides me with the guiding principles that I choose to embrace for balance and discernment, I can use my faith as a point of reference in accepting how, because of my baggage, anger, or "brain not required" addictive behaviors, I can be manipulated by handlers. This same faith discernment helps me to see through my own church's inconsistencies and hypocrisies.

The ability to acknowledge the philosophical premises upon which my perspectives are built is essential to appreciate the full implications of what I think I think. To the degree that I am merely parroting the position of my culture, class, religion, or "enlightened peers," this endeavor can appear daunting and be deemed unnecessary. If people do not question the lockstep allegiance to those to whom they have surrendered all critical consciousness, why would they even attempt to understand their own predigested reasons for voting against, arguing against, and demonizing the evil others? Negative political spots on TV and internet falsehoods can only take root in a society where people have allowed themselves to become undiscerning consumers who crave the bloodlust of campaign smears, even if truth is the first fatality.

If one also attempts to understand and appreciate the premises from which different people form their perspectives, it may be discovered that more concepts are held in common than not. As one unburies the origins of one's own premises, it provides an opportunity to more greatly understand both the differences and the similarities between contrasting perspectives and radically different conclusions without demonizing the other.

Here is a simple premise exercise of contrasting or incongruent ideas from which current issues are played like pawns for an underlying set of premises. Using the diagram of philosophical, ideological, or theological positions, you have the task of attempting to, as objectively as possible,

- name which of the following concepts that you identify with personally on an emotional or gut level
- identify the philosophies with which you objectively maintain some level of intellectual agreement
- name the ones that offend or even repulse you
- name as many current social conflicts that are extensions of each premise

The concepts are general premises that many of us function from without even being aware of it. The exercise can be done either by yourself or within the context of a small group dynamic. If the process occurs in a small group, there should be no commentary or debate on what someone else shares. Allow at least five minutes for people to check off or circle where their own personal beliefs are closest to from the list before the sharing begins. The emphasis is upon self-awareness and listening to others.

Reality is that which is.		Reality is what one believes.
Truth is relative.		Truth is universal.

Science reveals truth.	Religion reveals truth.		Spirituality reveals truth.	Truth doesn't exist.
Eugenics.	All *men* are created equal.		All people are created equal.	
Chauvinism.	Nationalism.	Patriotism.	Globalism.	Universalism.

The US Constitution is static.   The US Constitution is dynamic.

Christianity is foundational to America.   Capitalism is foundational to America.

We are caretakers of the earth.   The earth is ours to dominate.

Civil libertarianism.   The common welfare.

Sexual orientation is learned behavior.   Sexual orientation is genetic.

Religious fundamentalism.   Pluralism.

Objectivism.   Capitalism.   Socialism.

The ends justify the means.   The ends never justify. the means.

Freedom of religion.   Freedom from religion.   Freedom from government interference.

America: love it or leave it.   America: if you love it, live it.

Feminism.   Male chauvinism.

The diagram is not exhaustive in the least, so feel free to add your own isms. The following are examples of premises that stand on their own regarding how they have influenced both American thought and American policy through the years:

- predestination
- prosperity gospel
- manifest destiny
- altruism and spirituality being useless
- American interests being paramount
- social Darwinism
- humanism
- separation of church and state
- Protestant work ethic

- American dream
- America first

If utilized as a group process, the first round of shared reflection should be based on the first three reflections of the premise exercise. After everyone has had an opportunity to share, the group can attempt to take on number 4 together. Somebody can take notes or butcher paper can be used to organize your groups ideas. Debating and attempting to convert others to your way of thinking would be counterproductive as what you are trying to accomplish is to understand why you believe what you do and why others believe as they do. If we can get a handle on how we differ on the level of premises, it might help us to understand why we find ourselves at impasse after impasse on various issues.

I have found that some premises are nonstarters for relevant dialogue as they are based on divisiveness by definition. Eugenics and its proliferated versions, such as Arianism or white nationalism, are examples of such nonstarters. Some forms of fundamentalism also fall in this category as they exist mainly to distinguish between the *us* and the *them*. Other premises, though tainted by cultural and historical bias, can still be built upon to find common ground with those operating out of a completely different set of premises. If people of good will are willing to release their death grip of absolutist, all-or-nothing ideology, then it becomes possible to appreciate the other as an extension of one's own humanity. At this point, those who hold different perspectives are no longer the "other" but become a sister or brother with "whom I am united." This learned skill makes it possible to develop trust and mutual appreciation so that in an effort to find common ground, the baby is never thrown out with the bathwater, so to speak.

The four-step reflection can easily be used within the context of a small group dynamic, but it should not be shortchanged in an effort to serve the group process. One's personal reflections on the premise diagram is paramount in and of itself. You may notice that you may have intellectual adherence to some ideas with little or no emotional investment in them and vice versa. You may begin the very natural process of prioritizing philosophies and maybe even discover that some cherished ideas are completely incompatible with other revered concepts, though you may not have ever acknowledged the inconsistency within yourself. Facing up to and even accepting one's own distasteful compromises and rationalizations can create a landscape where one is so caught off guard by one's own hypocrisy that one hardly notices any longer the little "splinters" in the eyes of others.

Although it can be quite admirable to be passionate about particular issues that cut to the core of ones most basic beliefs, it must be understood that it is in the realm of emotions to the point of irrationality that well-intentioned people become identity politics "puppets" whose strings are pulled from the right and from the left. The nonreflective person in a "free" society can be manipulated to such a degree that the opinions that one parrots are merely the echo of propaganda by means of suggestion through the wide-open door of one's emotions. This cerebral hack via emotions is so efficient that it goes completely unnoticed. Think mob rule or lynching frenzy and you get the idea.

The bottom line is when individuals have allowed themselves to be so manipulated by biased media outlets, echo chamber websites, and even foreign operatives just to maintain the unthinking bias of identity politics, these same individuals may have in fact set themselves against the US Constitution and the common welfare of fellow Americans. There are some very good people who have been consumed by the extreme polarization that exists in the country and in the world who feel compelled to dig in their heels in the abandonment of truth, reason, and compassion. All who think differently from them are the enemy.

In the following chapters, we will closely examine how people with differing premises can find common ground. I will take some of the premise examples that I find foundational to my way of interpreting reality and hopefully illustrate how woefully inadequate our current one-dimensional cage is in constructively creating new avenues for finding solutions as opposed to attributing blame. Upon a cursory glance of where I stand on political issues, one might conclude that I suffer from multiple personality disorder as I am all over the place from the limited perspective of a left or right dichotomizing of thought. From the expanded examination of premise and underlying beliefs, much more is revealed to me and then to others where areas of commonness exist with others who hold opposing views on particular issues. From such common perspectives can trust and solidarity with others take form in the second dimension of common needs.

We need each other to pull the country out of this tailspin of hatred and mistrust, and it requires the sweat of working and pulling together where naive idealism will not be tolerated.

> For where jealousy and selfish ambition exist, there is disorder and every foul practice. But the wisdom from above is first of all pure, then peaceable, gentle, compliant, full of mercy and good fruits, without inconstancy or insincerity. And the fruit of righteousness is sown in peace for those who cultivate peace. (James 3:16–18 NAB)

FOUR

A SMATTERING OF PERSPECTIVE

I had intended to start this chapter with telling the story of the blind men and the elephant, but upon researching the origins of the story and realizing that there are in fact several versions with different emphases and different moral conclusions, I decided to use this evolving story line to tell its own story. The gist of the story is about a group of blind men who come upon an animal that they are completely unfamiliar with, an elephant. The man who touches the tail thinks it is like a rope. The one who touches the tusk thinks it is like a spear. The one who touches the trunk thinks it is like a large snake. The one who touches a leg thinks it is like a tree. The one who touches the side of the elephant thinks it is like a wall. The one who touches an ear thinks it is like a fan or broad leaf. They all draw different conclusions of what an elephant is, based upon their limited perspective or exposure.

Some versions take place in a town. Some take place in the jungle. Some versions have four men while others have six. Some have the king of the village call forth all the blind people in the village to participate in this experience. Some versions utilize monks as the blind men. A Buddhist version starts with how monks of another religion were arguing violently about something and report this to the Buddha, which gives him a segue into the story. Some versions continue the argument theme to teach their moral. Other versions use a resolution theme whereby the sharing of perspectives brings about a common understanding of the whole.

I am fascinated at how fans watching their favorite team either imagine or deny an infraction of some sort. Even with super slo-mo replays, the rabid fan almost can't see that the foot was or wasn't on the line, whether or not a foul was committed, etc. The devotion to the team essentially blinds some people to reality or fact. It isn't a mere disagreement with an official's or umpire's call as much as it is an inability to perceive clearly and/ or the creation of a mental block born from an irrational bias for one's team that distorts reality and creates an impasse for rational discussion. Now take this same tendency and apply it to our current political climate, and you will see how the failure of a two-party system is inevitable. The euphemism "reaching across the aisle" is based on an "us versus them" mindset to begin with and is somehow seen as noble and enlightened when the common welfare should always be the guiding principle for any deliberation by our representatives.

I encounter very few people who actually believe that our justice system works, yet so many people who are drawn into politics are lawyers. One might think that electing someone with an extensive legal background would be a good thing, but how does being groomed in our adversarial version of a justice process with an emphasis on winning become a constructive breeding ground for serving the common good, serving the country, serving the truth?

Now going back to the quandary of the misperceived elephant, it must be stated that my interpretation of the story is biased by the fact that I believe in objective truth. Not only objective truth but also in "capital T" Truth. The elephant is an elephant and an incorrect perception or a complete lack of perception does not change that. Yes, unless the tree falling in the forest is in the dead of space, its falling creates sound waves whether or not someone is there to hear them. For me to think otherwise would be as arrogant and historically inaccurate as saying that Columbus discovered the "New World."

If I am to fully integrate the significance of the story for me and also balance my belief in both an objective or knowable truth as well as Truth, I must have the humility and willingness to not only acknowledge my blind areas but to fully embrace them. If I am to perceive anything close to resembling the truth, I must in our culture of rugged individualism turn to the perceptions of others so that I might get the big picture. I need to listen to and be guided by others who have perceived not only a trunk but a tusk and a leg as well to be able to even admit that my perception is limited and therefore incomplete. But this is not possible if I lack trust because of my fear of the other, the enemy.

The alpha males and females will most likely view this as belly-up, exposed-throat weakness and will have to deal with their own knee-jerk reaction to even the possibility of such trust. Those who peddle fear will slam it as naïve, and those who are motivated by fear will have great trouble dealing with the unknown possibilities. Those who view themselves as "progressives" might have to unburden themselves of their self-righteousness just long enough to participate in a process that redefines what real progress is. Libertarians would have to come to the realization that the path to personal freedom and justice is a shared journey where the needs of the many cannot be dismissed.

The transition from single-dimension myopia to two-dimensional thinking is accompanied by a sense of what the greater good might be. When a common need arises, it can be fundamental in scope, such as group survival or advancement. This awareness can be the result of increased compassion through experiencing the needs of others arising from disaster and loss. In the first chapter, I referred to the unspoken language of second-dimensional processing as service. Think of it. First responders don't interrogate victims about their political views before saving them. Volunteers work side by side rescuing animals and cleaning devastated neighborhoods without the distraction of annoying town hall shouting about "important" matters. Firefighters and police risk their lives to save those in danger, not knowing anything about their race, culture, or immigrant status. The overwhelming need of victims in times of disasters, both large and small, drowns out the whining of ideological divisions so as to make them almost laughable.

The point here is not to gloss over real differences and the need for real conflict resolution, but just as the loss of a loved one or illness and impending death can transition a person to a place of reprioritizing their life in a more generative fashion, when a person is compelled by extreme conditions to serve the needs of others, there is no longer the false narrative of us and them. There remains a new appreciation for the sanctity of us— all of us. Those who have defined themselves by looking out for number 1 or the philosophy of "I got mine" might have the most difficult time in even considering the needs of the many as relevant at all. Of course, the current groupthink version of this is "America First" where many really believe that not questioning American policy and how it is implemented is in fact an act of patriotism.

As if transitioning to the second dimension of perception was not unusual enough, every now and then, we are challenged to take the next step where both response and unified purpose are for the most part indistinguishable. In my faith, every opportunity to receive Eucharist can be such a moment, and such moments can become a lifestyle and hopefully in time a way of being. Now if this seems radically inaccessible and metaphysical, as it were, please consider the passengers of Flight 93 who forced their own jet down on 9/11. Complete strangers considered their options in a relatively short time span and together chose the path of self-sacrifice for the good of fellow Americans. Abandoning self-interest in the awareness of the needs of others makes the transition into this third level of awareness and response almost like breathing.

Whatever diverging perspectives existed among the passengers of United Flight 93 as they boarded in Newark that morning, these perspectives were not an impediment to arriving at a unified vision and response. Their example and sacrifice have much to teach us if we will but move beyond memorializing and allow ourselves to be changed, really changed, by the honoring of their sacrifice. Yet as we—as individuals and as a culture— give in to our inner demons that hunger for division and fear, we succumb to the allure of the ringmasters of divisiveness, whether their name is bin Laden, Putin, or Trump.

Premise and Perspective

As a child in the sixties, I remember loving the song "Downtown" and thought it was so cool that Petula Clark would sing about my hometown's downtown area. Obviously, my conclusion was based upon the perspective of a child whose world up to that point was fairly small. As a very thin teenager, I made some awful judgments about obese individuals regarding will power and laziness and the usual bigoted opinions that come with ignorance. Not until I reached the age of fifty did I struggle with how difficult weight loss can be and repented of my previous position with great shame. Although I readily respect handicap parking places, I carried a subtle resentment about the inconvenience. Not until I had knee surgery a couple of years ago and severely broke an ankle recently did I gain the appropriate amount of respect and compassion for those who have lifelong physical struggles.

I still grapple with my knee-jerk aversion to tattoos, gauges, piercings, etc. and transition quite easily into the world of character judgment. It is good that I am not in a position for hiring people because I probably wouldn't let some individuals go beyond the initial interview—this from a "longhair." Go figure.

My biggest surprise in the area of wrong conclusions, bias, limited perspective, and myopic sensibilities dealt with my opinions of "White" people. In the sixties when I grew up, pretty much all my White friends had stay-at-home moms and dads who made more money than both of my working parents combined. They had so many advantages that the first time I saw a homeless White person, it didn't make any sense to me at all. Transitioning from a well-justified position regarding homeless Whites where I judged them as lazy and questioned their moral fiber to a place of compassion and nonjudgment was a long process. I didn't have a clue about Appalachian poverty or the effects of mental illness, drug addiction, or homelessness as a result of catastrophic illness or PTSD in many veterans. Whatever premise I was working from was flawed to the degree that I was almost completely blind. The question wasn't and isn't whether or not I had my head in the sand in defense of my ignorance but whether I would allow other perspectives to broaden my outlook and trust beyond my limited experience of people and of life in general. In each instance, my premise was wrong, my experience was narrow, and my conclusions were way off.

Love finds no joy in unrighteousness but rejoices in the truth. (1 Corinthians 13:6 NAB)

SECTI②N

THE ISSUES

FIVE

THE FLAG

I am the LORD your God, who brought you out
of the land of Egypt, out of the house of slavery.
You shall not have other gods beside me. You
shall not make for yourself an idol or a likeness
of anything in the heavens above or on the earth
below or in the waters beneath the earth; you
shall not bow down before them or serve them.

EXODUS 20:2–5

If one can believe it, the American flag has not always been a symbol of military service but of much more. The idea that thirteen diverse colonies with varied interests could be united by a common vision and ideals is a powerful symbol as represented by thirteen stars and thirteen stripes to form one flag. The symbolism of the flag has been crafted by means of propaganda and self-interest since the earliest versions were created. One thing for sure is the meaning of the flag as symbol has evolved along with its physical appearance.

We are all familiar with the story or legend of the flag sewn by Betsy Ross, a Philadelphia seamstress, and designed by New Jersey Congressman Francis Hopkinson. A variation of the story is that George Washington himself sketched out the flag with a circle of stars. The guidelines were established by the Continental Congress on June 14, 1777, and stated, "Resolved, that the flag of the United States be thirteen stripes, alternate red and white; that the union be thirteen stars, white in a blue field, representing a new constellation."

It was never clearer that the flag represented the "Union" than during the Civil War. The secession of the Southern states was never recognized as legitimate by the North and the flag used during that time contained all the stars representing the prewar Union and added West Virginia during the war itself. This same term *union* is foundational in both the Articles of Confederation and Perpetual Union as well as the Constitution of 1787.

Just as the Second Confederate Navy Jack and the Battle Flag of the Army of Northern Virginia, otherwise known as the Dixie flag, was never the flag of the Confederate States of America, so too the Stars and Stripes of the United States of America was never intended to be a symbol representing those who served in the military. This is simply historical fact. The "Rebel" flag has not been in continuous use since the Civil War. As a matter of fact, its use was popularized in the late 1940s and throughout the 1950s as a symbol of opposition to desegregation in the South. The meaning of the symbol is radically different depending on who you ask. For some people, it represents the "Lost Cause," while to others, it is simply a symbol of Southern pride and identity. To many, Dixie represents nothing more than racism and intolerance. Some people use this symbol alongside the Nazi flag to represent white supremacy. The common denominator between these different perspectives is an extreme emotional response to the issue.

In like fashion, the flag of the United States of America has had different symbology superimposed upon it. Its militarization, if you will, took place during WWI and was the result of sports promotion more than anything else. The dominant political momentum of isolationism reflected the sentiment of the populace at the time. The official position of "neutrality" kept the US out of the war. It may be that the first use of the term "America First" was during this period, though it had a radically different meaning then. President Woodrow Wilson used the phrase to indicate that America would be the first country to aid Europe once the war was over.

As history unfolded, the US finally did participate in the war. The daunting challenge was now to craft popular sentiment to transition to supporting the war. How does one make the transition from a popular isolationism to the support of a bloody world war? The answer is revealed in very clever propaganda. The whole idea of playing "The Star-Spangled Banner" at sporting events was part of an effort to bolster support for the troops sent to Europe. Incidentally, "The Star-Spangled Banner" did not officially become the national anthem until 1931. Just as the bawdy English bar song "To Anacreon in Heaven" had been appropriated for use as a patriotic anthem, the Stars and Stripes was now to become a symbol not of national unity but of support for those in the military.

Is it any wonder that some citizens who are unaware of the established meaning of the flag of the United States of America would equate not standing at attention during the national anthem as not only disrespectful to the country but to the men and women of the military as well? Without any life experience to the contrary, without any historical context which might shed new light on the issue, and without any desire to understand "the other" and their life experience, how can we but not have misunderstanding and division? At this point, the relevant issue is not about who has the most historically correct interpretation of the flag of the United States of America as much as it is about developing an awareness and appreciation for fellow citizens who have a different life experience of the flag and therefore a different interpretation of its meaning.

Yes, there can be more than one meaning given to a symbol as symbols tend to be fluid in what they represent and to whom. In 1942, we stopped pledging allegiance to the flag with the right hand outstretched toward the flag with the palm down as it was identical to the Nazi salute. For the previous forty years, the symbolism of that gesture was fairly innocuous—until it wasn't. The fact that there were once two pledges and the one which was formally adopted was written by Francis Bellamy, a Christian socialist and minister, is one of America's historical ironies. The fact that the same man who wrote the words "the land of the free," Francis Scott Key, was a slave owner is another crooked branch in the tree of American history.

Premise and Perspective

My journey to becoming a pacifist began during my childhood in the 1960s. I was a straight A student and believed what I was taught about American history, America's place in the world, and the ongoing war in Vietnam. I painted my room red, white, and blue, and I had my parents get me a flag-themed light cover for the bedroom light. By the fateful year of 1968, I was eight years old. We were a Walter Cronkite household, and when he chose to no longer function as a conduit for government policy and proceeded to share his reservations about the war effort, I was confused. The assassinations of Martin and Robert hit me hard, and then I was challenged to the core that October by Tommie

Smith and John Carlos at the Mexico City Olympic Games. In 1969, my big brother bought an album by Steppenwolf entitled *Monster*, which challenged all my beliefs about American history. I was never the same again after experiencing all these events in such a condensed span of time.

The seeds of doubt had been planted, and within the next few years, I had chosen to become a pacifist. The first day of summer vacation 1973, I took down my flag lamp and began to redo my bedroom. I was thirteen and had just completed the eighth grade. I had spent time learning about what our nation had done to the Native Americans and the economics of slavery and its lasting effects on America. At the same time, I developed a deep appreciation for the US Constitution and the ideals it represented. I became more aware of my social responsibility as a Catholic and my personal conscience was formed more and more by my spiritual reading. I no longer participated in the pledge at school, which created all kinds of grief for my parents.

As it became clear that the leaders of the country committed American lives to an unwinnable war through deception and political arrogance, my distaste for all things patriotic took root. The ignorance of those calling returning soldiers "baby killers" was only outdone by the ignorance of those yelling out, "America: love it or leave it!" The theoretical fear of dominoes falling was more important than the very real loss of life endured by tens of thousands of American families.

As a teenager, while at a friend's house, I encountered my first flag folded into a triangle and encased in a wooden display. I never met my friend's dad and often wondered how he died. As a musician and singer, I have had the honor to provide the music for many military funerals and graveside services. Each time is always just as moving as the first time. My sense of connection with the raw intimacy of the moment has had a profound impact on me and my sense of reverence for the families of those who serve our country.

I find myself intolerant of flag-themed clothing and political accoutrement such as may be found at conventions and the like. The disheartening videos of those who have chosen the incendiary practice of publicly stomping on the flag are tragic as these individuals are definitely part of the problem and not part of the solution. I do not consider myself patriotic in the sense that I cannot blindly defend American policy that has both economically and militarily oppressed people and nations around the world in the name of American interests. The concept of "America: love it or leave it" to me equals "America: right or wrong." My conscience does not allow for that kind of lukewarm compromise. I do not participate in the pledge as I have a God already. Thank you very much.

My sense of despair over the fading unity the flag represents for me helps me to discern between core American values and propaganda. My respect for the Constitution helps me to discern between common values and special interests or between the essence of American ideals and bumper sticker ideologies. If I had to distinguish between the difference in degree between respect given to the flag of the United States of America and the Constitution of the United States of America, I would have to maintain that the flag is a symbol and the Constitution is the reality.

Whatever respect is due to the flag exists only to the degree that we honor the Constitution. Wherever we fail to honor the freedom of all Americans, as in "with liberty, and justice for all," we fail to live and practice the citizenship of standing up for the dignity and rights of all Americans as laid out in the Constitution. Whenever the issue of patriotism and respect for the flag are politicized at the expense of these rights, know that it is a ruse to undermine the heart of the Constitution of the United States of America. The oaths of enlistment and the oaths of office are not to the flag. "I do solemnly swear (or affirm) that I will support and defend the Constitution of the United States against all enemies, foreign and domestic; that I will bear true faith and allegiance to the same." That kind of says it all.

SIX

BLACK LIVES MATTER

Being a Catholic in this day and age is not particularly easy. The sexual molestation scandal is very painful to endure, though only slightly as painful as the abuse endured by so many children. Even though 4 percent of priests have been accused of sexual impropriety during the last several decades, 96 percent of the priests are under suspicion for no reason at all. The most fascinating irony about this subculture is that it represents a coin that has two conflicting faces in our society. One face is that of a minority that has come under suspicion for just being who they are. The other face is that of men who exercise their power to shroud the actions of their members in secrecy, gather 'round the wagons to project a united front, and through denial and a complete lack of humility disregard any possible culpability of any of its members amid years of suffering by victims and their families.

We may never know how many people in authority at Penn State knew about the extracurricular activities of Coach Jerry Sandusky, who protected Dr. Richard Strauss at Ohio State as he sexually abused 177 young men over twenty years, or how many people in authority at US Gymnastics, US Olympics, and Michigan State had reason to suspect that Dr. Larry Nassar was systematically breaking trust and emotionally damaging so many victims. Was there a silent conspiracy for image's sake within the Boy Scouts of America as well? Even so, back at Penn State, young members of Beta Theta Pi, with so much to lose, were counseled so adroitly to follow the example of all the aforementioned adults and shroud the actions of their members in secrecy, gather 'round the wagons to project a united front, and through denial and a complete lack of humility disregard any possible culpability of any of its members. Timothy Piazza suffered a horrible and needless death and his family, I suppose, will continue to suffer for the rest of their lives.

The juxtaposition of this chapter to follow the previous chapter is purely intentional. Just as Malcolm Jenkins of the Philadelphia Eagles was attempting to convey via cue cards the intentional redirection of focus onto issues of patriotism and supposed disrespect for the flag, though merely a sideshow for the greater issue of the death of unarmed African American males at the hands of law enforcement officers, has become the center stage issue for much of White America. How in any rational world does that make sense? Deflection and misdirection have become the vehicles of nonaccountability.

Harking back to chapter 3, the image of rabid sports fans interpreting the calls of officials and umpires so radically different from the opposing fans goes so far beyond any simple interpretive bias so that some kind of warped confirmation bias must in fact be at play. This same bias phenomenon was so widely manifested in those who formed conflicting opinions upon viewing the infamous Rodney King tape. We see what we want to see and "interpret" accordingly. Attempting to arrive at truth never seems to enter this kind of process so discernment is disregarded altogether.

"Sometimes, a cigar is just a cigar" reminds us that any

predefined parameters for interpretation of one's experiences, which becomes the only channel through which one's perceptions are filtered, can lead to grave errors in judgment. The Brett Kavanaugh hearings are a most ludicrous recent example of this impairment. How can millions of people draw such contrasting conclusions based on partisan interests and perspective? Is the truth that irrelevant as long as I outmaneuver the opposing side? Do die-hard Republicans completely disregard the very real possibility that Kavanaugh perjured himself on several points and revealed a deep-seated bias against and contempt for Democrats? Do Democrats not care that there is a very real possibility that Kavanaugh is in fact innocent of the allegations made against him and that is why there was a dearth of corroborating evidence? One wonders if even DNA evidence, if it had existed, would be enough to change people's conclusions.

In addressing the Black Lives Matter issue, the essential self-knowledge to have revolves around preconceived ideas and a lack of trust. There exist young people who are raised to not only fear law enforcement officers but to hate them as well. There are officers who racially profile as a matter of course. There are violent individuals who intentionally assassinate members of law enforcement. As in all professions, there are individuals wearing a badge who should be weeded out from their departments, by their departments themselves. Mistrust and preconceived ideas about the other affect each of the aforementioned scenarios negatively and are the kindling upon which the fire of divisiveness burns hot. Constructive dialogue can't begin until the issues of trust and bias are taken head on. One way to do this is to put oneself into the other's shoes.

Without getting overwhelmed with the myriad explanations for Black-on-Black crime, I can't imagine how it must really feel for a law enforcement officer to patrol any impoverished neighborhood in the country, which is predominately Black and has a high murder rate. I would probably be more vigilant and cautious at the same time. I might have an elevated heart rate and increased adrenalin production kicking in before I encountered any crime at all, but therein lies the problem. The instinctual survival response of my body will have already skewed my ability to discern rationally and objectively. The foundation to exonerate and explain away anything that happens after that has been laid so that my classic catch-all defense would be "I feared for my life." This justification construct exists before the first encounter, before any crime is committed, and before the cop cam or the cell phone videos commence.

From opposing perspectives, one might conclude that the obvious impasse is a lose-lose proposition from the start, but that happens only when we allow ourselves to dehumanize the "other." If my parent or spouse were a law enforcement officer who worked a crime-ridden area, I would probably have a similar anxiety level as a member of a military family whose loved one is deployed to a dangerous war zone. Even when the assignment is "noncombative," such as a training assignment in Afghanistan, the constant threat of "trainees" firing on American personnel is very real and not that dissimilar from individuals targeting cops just because they are cops. Also, the deployment is not a year or so at a time but is in fact a lifestyle. Do I fully appreciate the human toll on the families of law enforcement officers, and do I even care?

If I lived in a neighborhood where children were gunned down and friends and relatives were murdered and survival considerations entailed whether or not a child can walk home safely from school, my worldview would probably reflect the dysfunction of my environment. Combine this with unarmed citizens of these United States of America being shot and killed by law enforcement. Just imagine the whole gamut of emotions one might feel, from despair and hopelessness to rage and paranoia, from fear and powerlessness to bitterness and vengeance. Every situation where an unarmed African American male is killed by a law enforcement officer adds gasoline to a raging fire, no matter where it happens in the country.

Both scenarios and every scenario in between exist as a challenge for more empathy and not as justification for division. The loss of life and the suffering that pours forth are a call to compassion and mutual understanding if we would but seek true accountability all around and seek true solutions instead of casting blame. In this instance, the difference between casting blame and true accountability is as simple as the difference between being preoccupied with the splinter in someone else's eye and examining the plank in my own eye.

In the most basic of terms, this means that law enforcement agencies need to retrain like they mean it and get rid of those officers who are only out to "protect and to serve" themselves. They are a small minority, but they perpetuate the negative public image that is applied to all law enforcement. There can be zero tolerance for lying on behalf of fellow officers. De-escalation of potentially dangerous situations needs to be balanced against noncompliance to police orders. Stress/anxiety training needs to be ongoing so that officers do not interpret all situations from a survival instinct mode yet still maintain the highest awareness of potential danger for everyone in the vicinity. If law enforcement agencies really want to prioritize the essence of what "to protect and to serve" really means, then token sensitivity training that is imposed on officers is not enough. Police unions need to begin to be part of the solution and not an impediment to the process.

For those living in crime-ridden neighborhoods, the accepted norms of behavior need to be challenged and debunked. Why have out-of-wedlock births and fatherless families become the norm in so many communities? This factor alone has a direct correlation to poverty and crime. Why is the "gangsta" image glorified? Why are peaceful demonstrations allowed to be infiltrated by common thugs who look to create rioting and looting of neighborhood businesses? Why has looting become acceptable behavior once it has started? Why are some children raised to not only fear but to hate all law enforcement?

If law enforcement needs to take a hard look at how they have failed to serve their communities and work toward a more just application of the law for all citizens, then how much more do communities of color need to stop perpetuating a victim's mindset by blaming others and instead take their communities back. The experience of stable families and learning the value of hard work at an honest job are not realities that are foreign to minority communities, but these same values are challenged at every turn in some communities due to both economic and social realities. The point is it is not a simple matter of blaming cops or blaming crime-ridden communities but a matter of supporting both as societal priorities.

Premise and Perspective

My father was a naturalized citizen from Torreón Coahuila, Mexico, and as a teacher and coach, he was a very strict disciplinarian. My response to all adults and all people of authority was always "Yes, sir" and "Yes, ma'am." We didn't really have "the talk" about encountering police as it was a foregone conclusion that I would always show them respect. We did though have the talk about how we would speak English almost exclusively at home so that I would be able to defend myself competently if the need arose.

As a teen and later as a young man, I was stopped repeatedly by law enforcement for no reason at all. I was a Hispanic male with long hair and frumpy clothes; I still fit that description incidentally. With each encounter, as they began to question why I was where I was, where I was going, etc., I would ask them why they stopped me. I would ask if they saw me commit a crime, if I fit the description of a suspect, or if someone reported me as suspicious. Essentially, I would insist that they indicate any probable cause for stopping me. When they didn't answer, I would respond something to the effect of "Thank you, sir. Now if you don't mind, I'll be on my way." I would then turn around and continue with what I was doing or where I was going. I am not sure that I would respond in the same way in this age of absolute compliance for no particular reason at all and the accelerated rush to deadly force because of noncompliance.

More recently, I became acutely aware of my own biases regarding law enforcement when I was called to jury selection. The case involved someone who was allegedly belligerent and a law enforcement officer who allegedly got physical while attempting to restrain the individual. There was a question of whether or not excessive force was used. It was general information about the case. It was then mentioned that another police officer came upon the scene and was going to testify on behalf of the first officer. I was uncomfortable after a few minutes and stewed in that discomfort for a little bit until I realized that I could not be an objective juror. I raised my hand and told the judge that I would automatically assume that any officer who testified on behalf of another officer was simply lying to protect the other officer. There was a low murmur of disapproval among my fellow prospective jurors and then the judge asked if anyone else would automatically assume that a law enforcement officer would lie for another officer to please stand. Approximately half of the attendees stood up.

This whole turn of events was self-revelatory in that I hadn't ever confronted this bias in myself. I was even more surprised to see how many others believed as I did, even though some may have simply seen an opportunity to be dismissed. I have friends in law enforcement and others who are retired cops. My granddaughter's godfather is a young cop, and we are so proud of him. If I, who has never been arrested, who refuses to jump to conclusions regarding accusations against law enforcement, and who strongly believes that too broad a brush has been applied to law enforcement because of the callous actions of a very small minority, have such a lack of trust in the testimony of one cop for another, what is the solution?

So one of my preconceived biases is in fact a lack of trust. I don't trust the testimony of police officers. I don't trust the justice system to even attempt to find the truth. I don't trust the current system and process. What I see is men who exercise their power to shroud the actions of their members in secrecy, gather 'round the wagons to project a united front, and through denial and a complete lack of humility disregard any possible culpability of any of its members in the midst of years of suffering by victims and their families. I see a societal cancer where protecting "our own" in this instance weighs far more than "to protect and to serve."

To make matters worse, I had a terrible experience with El Paso's finest a couple of years ago when I spoke at a city council meeting requesting the dismissal of the chief of police. While I attempted to address the council, I was booed and heckled by police union members who filled the room in support of their chief. To give some background to this climax of various events, it involved the organization of a community gathering in support of Black Lives Matter that would be held in downtown El Paso,

Texas. The event had been scheduled for at least a few weeks and unfortunately fell on the Sunday after police officers were intentionally ambushed and singled out and where five officers were murdered and nine others were injured in Dallas during a Black Lives Matter march. The day after the Dallas murders, after a press conference, a reporter asked Police Chief Greg Allen what he would have to say to the people attending the upcoming Black Lives Matter event. His response was

> Black Lives Matter, as far as I'm concerned, is a radical hate group; and for that purpose alone, I think the leadership of this country needs to look at little bit harder at that particular group. The consequences of what we saw in Dallas is due to their efforts.

The fact is Micah Xavier Johnson, the Dallas murderer of police officers, acted on his own. He didn't much care for Black Lives Matter but had been on websites that advocated the killing of police. The BLM organizers of the vigil here in El Paso immediately included the names of the murdered officers in the vigil for that Sunday.

The following is the text from my presentation before the El Paso City Council:

Call to the Public Item
City Council Meeting
July 12, 2016
Presenter: Roland A. Guerrero

Ladies and gentlemen of the city council, Mayor Leeser, I thank you for the opportunity to address you regarding a very pressing concern for many in our city. I am referring to the inflammatory statements made recently by our current city chief of police, Chief Greg Allen.

In a critical time when trust and open dialogue are at a premium in our cities and the tendency toward polarization and preconditioned attitudes and biases against one another is so prevalent in our society, it is beyond unfortunate that a well-respected representative of the City of El Paso, in an official capacity as chief of police, chose to engage in inflammatory rhetoric and accusation concerning members of the Black Lives Matter movement.

The revelation of such an angry bias against members of the citizenry of our nation coupled with the outrageous accusation of culpability in the terroristic murder of five police officers and the wounding of at least nine officers and two civilians recently in Dallas requires a thoughtful examination of whether or not Chief Allen is truly capable of engendering the trust necessary in this critical time as the chief of police for our city.

I as a citizen of El Paso have lost all confidence in Chief Allen's ability to uphold his oath as a police officer. I would hope that Chief Allen would have the humility to recognize the degree of damage he has brought upon the image of the already vilified men and women in blue who serve us every day and that he would recognize that he does not exemplify the cool-headed objectivity required to lead the police force and should therefore submit his resignation. In the event that following dialogue between Chief Allen and the city he refuses to resign, I respectfully request that steps be taken to replace Chief Allen as the chief of police for the City of El Paso.

I have no agenda—political, personal, or otherwise. If the vast majority of our police officers adhere to the same bias as Chief Allen, which I don't believe they do, then we have a very serious problem to address in the retraining of our officers. If in fact the vast majority of our police officers do not harbor this same predisposition and accusatory attitude toward the people they serve, then Chief Allen does not honestly represent the men and women who put their lives on the line for us. In either case, Chief Allen has shown his true colors and this cannot be undone.

The predisposition of a police officer against any group of people will affect his or her emotional interpretation of the threat risk in every encounter as we have painfully seen this past week. The predisposition against police officers because of the lack of trust and generalizations which don't encourage respect for our officers engenders polarization and fear. This is not an issue of political correctness or possible censure of a city employee. Chief Allen has expressed a polarized view and no longer has the objectivity necessary to perform his duties. He has become part of the problem.

In light of the tragedy that occurred in Dallas, it would seem normal for any police officer to feel the loss personally under such stress and for emotions to run high. I can't fault Chief Allen for this. But there's the rub. At times of great stress, we are often pushed to our limits and our preconceived judgments come to the surface fueled by anger, fear, and adrenalin and greatly affect our judgment in a crisis situation. What one says and how one responds at the moment of stress and crises can be a direct reflection of one's deepest held opinions of others. This remains as true for the individual in the position of the chief of police as it is for the cop on the street. Therein lies the heart of the matter.

When the booing and the heckling by the police union members got loud, I simply did not attempt to speak over them but waited on and off throughout my presentation in exercising my right to speak in open forum to the city representatives. Because of my pausing, I was not allowed to continue as I had reached the time limit allowed to address the city council. I was the first presenter that morning, and without exception, those who spoke in support of Chief Allen were allowed to finish their presentations past their allotted time. The whole experience was quite disillusioning for me and represented the foundation upon which systemic injustice permeates all levels of government and where police unions flex their influential muscles to intimidate spineless city council members who are more concerned about reelection than justice. If a school principal or superintendent had made such glaringly false and biased allegations about a segment of the student population, the response would be swift.

The irony of it all and the blessing is that the Black Lives Matter event itself was very uplifting. Most of the organizers were from NMSU in Las Cruces, New Mexico, and UTEP, and the speakers were eloquent with moving stories of the loss of loved ones at the hands of law enforcement and the many experiences of racial profiling throughout their lives. They conscientiously chose to have a stationary protest so as to mitigate the possibility of violence and looting that can occur with a march. The only part of the protest that was out of place was that some old Black Panther member and a Brown Beret weaseled themselves onto the roster of speakers toward the end with hateful ranting and uncontrolled anger. The young organizers were finally able to regain control of the microphone after several attempts. That old, tired militancy was so foreign to the vibe of the rest of the evening.

Reflecting on that experience after a few years, I have come to realize that the bias of "our men in blue can do no wrong" is very deeply seated in line with "our troops can do no wrong" and "our country can do no wrong." Any voice to the contrary is viewed as disloyal. It doesn't matter how much one actually supports the police if that support is not absolute and at all times.

This alone drives the rhetoric to an extreme pole that doesn't allow for informed dialogue. When fueled by very real bigotry toward minorities, our cultural prejudices can create several different levels of justice and even a policing class that is above the law.

Upon reflecting on other people's perceptions of African Americans and the cultural or learned prejudices of some people, I draw upon my childhood experiences. In the 1960s, my mom was a track coach, and both the boys and girls track teams at Stephen F. Austin High School where she coached were dominant. At one celebratory party at our house, which was a block and a half from the school, team members showed up to the door throughout the evening. There were no Blacks living in our neighborhood, which prompted a next-door neighbor to ask about all the "jigaboos" who were showing up to our house. I had no idea what was being asked as I had never even heard the term.

On another occasion, the next-door neighbors on the other side of the house left me speechless. I must have been around ten or so when I accepted the job of washing their camper and truck every time they came home from a camping trip and I liked having the spending money. Well, on one occasion, I must have done a great job as my neighbor praised me for getting the camper "as white as a nigger's heel." I had no reply. I think I was in shock over what I had just heard. How does a ten-year-old reply to an adult in that situation? What happens to children who are raised in that environment all their lives? What happens when those same children become law enforcement officers?

I have never lived in a ghetto or in the projects and my Black friends growing up were middle class suburbanites just like me. I didn't then and probably still don't appreciate the reality of feeling trapped by crime, drugs, and gangs. I own that ignorance, but it does not excuse me from standing in solidarity with Black

Lives Matter. I have to ask, "What if that were my child?" because if I don't, then I probably don't believe that we are all created equal or in justice for all.

Though I admittedly have only contempt for police unions, I don't harbor fear of law enforcement officers. I believe they are underpaid, especially in my city of El Paso. I believe that in this unstable time of both domestic terrorism and the threat of terrorism from abroad, our law enforcement officers need every available advantage to do their job well, and this includes the acquisition of military vehicles and hardware. Who is better trained with feet on the ground than local law enforcement? The use of these acquisitions should be considered judiciously though and utilized only in extreme situations where conventional intervention and de-escalation have been attempted and have not been effective.

I have to confront the areas where my trust is worn very thin. My issue with police unions probably has something to do with my lack of respect for teachers' unions. My bias about teachers' unions is that they are really good about fighting for people who should never have become teachers to begin with. Every school has a minority of teachers who show up to school at the last minute, are the first ones to leave without taking any work home, and who complain the loudest. These individuals have no passion for teaching and no love or concern for the children they teach. This kind of minority exists in nearly every profession. The personality types that manifest characteristics of power, dominance, and control have no place in law enforcement and hurt the reputation of their fellow officers. They have to be excised, not defended.

With this said, there exist several more parallels between law enforcement and the teaching profession. Both are expected to address social issues well beyond the scope of their professions as more parents refuse to parent or just don't know how. More families are broken through divorce, drug abuse, and physical and sexual abuse than ever before, and where society has failed, somehow law enforcement officers and teachers are required to fill in the gaps and then be scapegoated when they are not able to. The most striking parallel at present is the "defund the police" movement that demands the dismantling of policing agencies without the input or active participation of those who will be most affected: the police themselves. Teachers have been victimized for years by well-meaning political entities who desired to establish measurable levels of accountability in order for the gods of the blame game to be satisfied. There was never any real desire for educational reform as teachers were required to jump through more hoops with mandated testing and newer new programs while being stripped of instruction time and ever precious preparation time. As a result, the poorer teachers who have mastered the art of the "dog and pony show" deflect true accountability and many of the most gifted and passionate teachers have left the profession out of profound discouragement.

In our need to attribute blame as a result of systemic racism in law enforcement that results in the death of unarmed people of color, we target the ones who are serving us and do not even try to look more deeply at the root causes and justifications for racism. We need to learn from our mistakes and not throw out the baby with the bathwater. The "bathwater" regarding policing is systemic racism mixed with rage and control issues that have made noncompliance a capital offense.

As White men in places of power refuse to acknowledge that systemic racism exists, the task of communities of color and of those burdened by economic disenfranchisement need to communicate their lived experiences to those same men. I can deal with the fact that as recently as the 1970s I was refused service in a restaurant, probably because I was with a White girl. What I have difficulty with is that my son Benjamin, while working on his master's degree at NYU, was racially profiled just a few years back as part of the "stop and frisk" policy of the NYPD. The reality is haunting for minorities and particularly for Black Americans.

No, not my son. It can't be happening still to my son.

To bring this chapter full circle, I as a Catholic have to confront the predatory priest issue head on and not blindly defend priests just because I am Catholic. Even though I acknowledge that the Catholic church is an easy target in the press and that centuries-old prejudice and stereotypes against Catholics are commonplace in contemporary cinematic themes, I must honestly and objectively respond to the harm done to children at the hands of priests in my church. I go back to this comparison because there exists in my estimation a bias against law enforcement where context is completely ignored and judgment is made on the basis of a snippet of video. Officers are tried and convicted in the court of public opinion long before the facts of a case are revealed. I have also known priests who were falsely accused and were ultimately vindicated. With this said, I also believe that the greatest culpability in the Catholic Church lies with those in places of authority who tried to sweep the scandal under the rug and therefore put more children at risk through lateral moves of predatory priests.

It is out of love and devotion to my church that the discernment becomes crystal clear that children need to be protected at all costs and that real consequences need to be meted out to both the perpetrators and the enablers in the hierarchy of the church. By the same token, authentic support for all the incredible men and women in law enforcement does not entail turning a blind eye to heinous acts by police officers. The badge is not tarnished by the truth but is held in greater esteem when true justice for all is the ultimate goal of all parties. Conversely, the badge is allowed to be dragged in the mud when bad cops go scot-free without so much as a slap on the hand. Society suffers when justice is abandoned because some believe that standing behind police interests at all costs takes precedent over protecting and serving. Countless bishops believed they were protecting the interests of the church by gathering 'round the wagons in the name of protecting the church. They failed to acknowledge that all those abused children were the church that needed protecting. The unarmed citizen who ends up dead as a result of deadly force by police is the same citizen who needed protecting and serving.

Even though I have to confront my trust issues, my response to law enforcement will continue to be "Yes, sir" and "Yes, ma'am." I will maintain that level of respect because I believe that law enforcement officers deserve my respect and cooperation for them to do their jobs well. They put their lives on the line for me, my family, and my community. With this said, I can't allow myself to be caught in the false dichotomy between conservatives and liberals or Republicans versus Democrats. The common interests of police policing themselves and increasing opportunities for positive interactions between law enforcement and the communities they serve are not political footballs but opportunities to build bridges of trust. For us to successfully focus together on mutual accountability to find real solutions and not just political Band-Aids, we must abandon our cultural predilection for casting blame with every knee-jerk emotion that comes with it. Solutions will only be found once the blame game has ceased.

We stand at the threshold of casting off the chains that can only serve antagonism, the polarized thinking of "us and them." When the day arrives that law enforcement no longer stands apart as above the law, when the communities of color can remember that bigoted generalizations are always wrong, even those which frame all police officers as the enemy, then maybe we will all see that we are members of the same community. We are us, and they are us.

> Do everything without grumbling or questioning, that you may be blameless and innocent, children of God without blemish in the midst of a crooked and perverse generation, among whom you shine like lights in the world. (Philippians 2:14–15 NAB)

SEVEN

PRO-LIFE, PRO-CHOICE, PRO-FEAR, AND ACCUSATION

What issue is more contentious and volatile than the issue of reproductive rights juxtaposed against the rights of unborn children? On the single-dimensional line between the extremes of abortion clinic bombers and murderers of abortion providers on one end and the multibillion-dollar abortion industry with its lobbyists on the other end, to which pole are you closer, and what if you are wrong? Perhaps the rights one fights for are not as absolute and the world is not so black and white as the rhetoric on both sides would lead one to believe.

If the talking points on either side are defined by fear and murder, and the images range from coat hangers to grisly abortions, there is nothing left to do but attack the humanity of the "others" and demonize them to the end. But what if this impasse is nothing more than a monstrous false dichotomy? What if the ability to appreciate some varying shades of gray from a different vantage point, say a second dimension from the line and possibly even a third dimension, is needed to appreciate the humanity of the others?

I propose a few questions that might punch some holes in the self-righteousness of the extremes, including the following:

- How is it that one can claim to be pro-life yet not have a problem with one's pro-life candidate or administration supporting a despotic regime in the murder of over ten thousand civilians in Yemen?

- How is it that a pro-choice advocate can fight for laws that protect full gestation and hatching of endangered sea turtles and not recognize that unborn children perhaps might have those same rights?

- How can a person have such intense regard for unborn children and in the importance of family yet be so dismissive of the needs of children who are born into poverty and whose families suffer both social and economic injustice?

- If we have come so far as a species, how is it that men dehumanized women and children with the word *chattel*; slaveowners dehumanized real people with the term *soulless pagans*; Nazis dehumanized Jews, homosexuals, and the physically and mentally impaired with the concept of *inferior races*; and the voiceless unborn child is dehumanized when he or she is referred to as a *fetus*?

- How is it that a political posturing that is supposedly pro-life does not also recognize the dignity of those on death row, some of whom are innocent, or the rights of immigrants fleeing persecution in their country and seeking asylum in the United States?

- Are those pro-choice advocates who also champion civil rights issues aware that the highest rate of abortions per thousand women is in the African American community and that the second highest rate is in the Hispanic community? Also, where is the line drawn in the development of the child when the decriminalization of infanticide due to the effects of postpartum depression is gaining support in this country in reflection of legislation already on the books in England? In 2015, Black women accounted for 36 percent of abortions even though Blacks represent 13.4 percent of the US population, according to Centers for Disease Control and Prevention figures released in November 2019. In New York City, there were nearly three thousand more abortions than live births among non-Hispanic Black women, according to state health department figures.

The fact that the United States is the most expensive country in the world to have a baby even with insurance and can cost a family or single mother anywhere from $10,000 to $30,000 without insurance, deeply affects a woman's "freedom of choice" as a result of a broken medical system. Using the well-worn social justice allegory of retrieving wounded people from the river, both extremes battle over ideological differences on how best to treat the wounded, but neither side is even remotely addressing the issue of where the bodies are coming from.

Now that we have both sides adequately defensive, let's take a closer look at the basic premise conflicts that exist. The idea of rights versus rights asks us to more closely examine the concepts of personal rights or fundamental rights. The questions surrounding the rights of the individual and the responsibilities or rights of a society continue to remain polarized in this country.

From the perspective of reproductive rights, the historical fact that men have defined and/or limited the rights of women for thousands of years must be taken into account. The widow had no rights apart from her husband. If a man beat his wife and children in his own castle, it was understood that he was free to do as he pleased with his property. These same historical underpinnings are still represented in societal norms every time a woman is not believed, every time the victim is victimized, every time a glass ceiling isn't challenged, every time that the risk of pregnancy as part of the workforce is viewed as a liability and not a blessing, and every time a little girl is not encouraged that she can strive to dream and become whomever she wants to be without limitations. As a man, if I don't own up to my participation in this distorted construct, even if it only meant silently taking "advantage" of the cultural "advantages" afforded me by virtue of being male, then I am the oppressor.

In a nutshell, any "pro-lifer" who does not support equal pay for equal work, paid maternity leave for couples, affordable day care, fair treatment for pregnant women at work, workplace accommodations for breastfeeding employees to pump at work, unbiased educational opportunities for all children, and a revamping of a justice system that favors the rights of predatory men over the rights of women is not credible. The necessary trust that conveys a value for women and their rights is essential; otherwise, dialogue is impossible.

This does not mean that people will change their hard-held positions, but it provides an opportunity to appreciate the humanness and the common aspirations of those whose voices must be heard in the midst of systemic oppression—times ten for minority women.

From the perspective of the rights of the unborn child, one must seriously consider why thirty-eight states have fetal homicide laws on the books if in fact the unborn child is not a person. This also applies to manslaughter charges when an unborn child is killed in a car accident. One must also consider a parallel between the argument of slave owners and their property and the argument of "my body" by not having to deal with the rights of the slave or the fetus. Relegating the slave to nonpersonhood meant that the only "legal" questions that slave owners needed to address were in the realm of property rights. Relegating the unborn child to the designation of fetus allows for a myopic emphasis on perceived personal rights. One would think that if social justice principles were applied objectively, then the voicelessness of the slave, the woman, the economically disenfranchised, or the unborn child represents the very nature of oppression.

Consequently, can there be a feminism that considers the rights of unborn little girls who might grow up to be governors, senators, or the next president? Can there be a feminism that does not involve the litmus test of a pro-choice position? Throughout history, the negative cycle of the oppressed becoming the oppressor seems to be unavoidable, particularly from the male-dominated tendency for violence and subjugation to the exclusion of cooperation and compassion. Those people who sincerely believe in reproductive rights must consider that ideological rights can never be more important than people or, in this case, a class of defined "unpeople." They must consider that not all pro-life positions are exclusively antiabortion focused or sexist in principle and practice.

As to personal rights weighed against a social moral imperative or the needs of the many so to speak, the assertion of absolute rights and the sacred cow of all-or-nothing political positions also makes dialogue impossible. If the equation of being a Democrat or feminist equals supporting the absolute right to abortions, does it hold that supporting the Second Amendment equals supporting the absolute right to owning AR-15s or parental rights equals defending an absolute right not to vaccinate their children? Such all-or-nothing reasoning is permanently stuck on the polarization line with little if any chance of or desire for real solutions.

Many of the current Republican positions and legislative actions are contrary to the gospel of Jesus Christ and church social teachings. Being against abortion is the one-issue lynchpin that seems to override all other considerations where the pro-life "ends" justify the "means" of voting for Trump. If being a Republican or pro-lifer is a consistent position, then do the ends justify the means as long as "conservative" judges are appointed by conservative administrations even though many poor expectant mothers and their unborn and born children do not have affordable access to health care and where Black babies are 2.5 times more likely to die than White babies before the age of one? Do the ends justify the means even though racism, sexism, xenophobia, and hate crimes are on the increase as a result of inflammatory rhetoric from conservative politicians and pundits? Do the ends justify the means when deniers of global warming use pro-life positions to get elected and then turn around and dismantle environmental protections that were established for the welfare of all people, especially generations to come? Do the ends justify the means when expectant mothers face the penalty of a murder conviction as a result of having an abortion? To paraphrase 1 Corinthians 13, if I appoint only pro-life judges and legislate successfully to eliminate legal abortion, but have not love ...

In order to build trust and be in relationship with individuals who have opposing points of view that probably are not going to change, it takes a concerted effort to keep one's eye on the ball of common values and shared concerns. The temptation to demonize the "other" is always present and is much too easy. The willingness to seek these relationships and to abandon absolute, "sacred cow" devotion to *how* an issue is to be addressed is the threshold to two-dimensional vision.

In counseling, reflecting what one is hearing the other person say can be invaluable. It is a learned skill and participants need to have their defensiveness in check. Both from conversations and attentive listening, this is what I perceive that each side is hearing from the other, which in turn breaks down trust.

Many pro-choice advocates receive these messages from pro-lifers, intended or not. The experience of women is irrelevant. Women don't matter. Giving birth to children is the only thing that gives a woman meaning or significance. Women don't need to be paid as much as men because they should be staying home with the children anyway and equal pay will pull them away from their womanly duties at home. "We" know what is best for you, and you certainly are not capable of making serious decisions on your own, for yourself. The suffering and emotional turmoil of women and girls in unwanted pregnancies is insignificant in that they created the situation as a direct result of their deficient moral character. You don't matter.

How is a young woman not to interpret this brand of reasoning as anything other than a defining of the role of a woman to be "barefoot and pregnant in the kitchen"?

On the flip side, many pro-lifers receive these messages from pro-choice advocates, intended or not. We are more evolved than you and your primitive religious beliefs. Motherhood is a definite disadvantage and should be treated as such. Our sense of womanhood is vastly superior to yours. Women who have children and choose to stay home with them are brainwashed. Pro-lifers are inherently ignorant and are living in the past. We refuse to work with anyone on any women's issues if they do not support reproductive rights as we define them, and until you think like us, believe like us, and march in unwavering lockstep to our one issue, then we have no use for you. You don't matter.

Now the next part of the dynamic is a serious reflection

on "You heard what?" This self-reflection needs to take place before the predictable "I didn't say that or mean to say that. You completely misunderstood." What is to be avoided at all costs is the defensive response "You are just twisting the meaning of what I said." To cut to the chase, one has to be aware of the subtext implicit in one's position.

To reiterate, these hypothetical messages are expressions of my perception of how these two groups talk past or at each other, and because of a deep sense of accusation and a lack of trust, true dialogue is almost impossible once the posturing has begun and the lines in the sand have been drawn. There is a world of hurt on each side where in a male-dominated world, being dismissive of the opposition's wounds comes easily. Women need not emulate the control-centered or power-centered priorities of men but could in fact bring their unique strengths of compassion, nurturing, and the valuing of relationships to the fore where the person always takes precedence over the issue or the male fixation over the "solution." Many women in both political parties are in fact against the killing of the unborn, yet they have no voice as a result of male-dominated polarization.

From a political perspective, what would the polarized parties do with a candidate who didn't fit their mold? Imagine a Republican who believed in the rights of the unborn child but saw *Roe v. Wade* as a decided issue. Therefore, fighting for "pro- life" conservative justices would be a nonstarter and the only considerations would be how qualified and how impartial a judge this person would be. Imagine that this individual also believed in equal pay for women, maternity leave for couples, affordable day care, and the threat of global warming and supported the "Me Too" movement. Imagine a Democrat who was on the record as pro-choice but saw no value in promoting late-term abortions and who had a keen sense that using federal dollars for abortions would create greater division in the country. And out of a real sensitivity for how strongly people believe on this issue, he or she could not in conscience go along with such measures. Imagine that there were pro-life, Catholic Democrats who supported all the aforementioned rights for women and also united to caucus for keeping the Hyde Amendment just as it is written. Any of these mythical people would be individuals who think beyond and through the sacred cow, absolutist quagmires, and because of the current state of affairs in both parties, they would probably have to run as an independent.

Premise and Perspective

As a Catholic firmly rooted in my faith family, I believe that life begins at conception. That is probably one of the only things I have in common with the politicized pro-life movement. The ways in which I differ from your average pro-lifer are many and radical to say the least. I believe that the "issue" of the dignity of life is a spiritual reality that all people do not share and it will not be "solved" through political means.

Aren't there still limits to what positions are acceptable for US citizens? I don't believe that the United States is a Christian nation, if it ever was, but I do believe that the country is in a post-Christian cultural shift. This leaves vestiges of cultural religious belief and practice that are not particularly Christian or moral in any way. This allows for Americans to be racist and still be either pro-choice or pro-life. This allows Americans to be sexist and still be pro-choice or pro-life. This allows Americans to embrace the moral injustices of capitalism in order to maintain their consuming lifestyles and still be pro-choice or pro-life. From my perspective, no moral high ground coexists with hypocrisy.

I also diverge significantly from popular feminist thinking in that for me, it is not enough to emulate the oppressive, power-centered priorities of men but to cast them off completely and share the perspectives and insights of women and not as surrogate men in a male-dominated construct. It isn't about playing the game; it's about getting rid of the game entirely.

The strengths I value in women, I have observed in my mother, my wife, and my daughter. These strengths draw on the potential of relationships and process, of compassion and firmness, and of vision and realizing dreams. These strengths exercise the value of cooperation over competition and do not shy away from extending a hand up to other women regardless of ideology or race or culture.

The sad reality is that since *Roe v. Wade* in 1973 and the failure of the ratification of the ERA, women have been pitted against each other by means of the ideological battles of men. To think that decades later, women still make only eighty cents for every dollar earned by men is absurd. The fact that most medical studies are performed on men and then applied to women's health is ludicrous. We are so proud of ourselves that women have set an all-time high for holding seats in Congress—a whopping 19 percent from a pool of 50.6 percent of the US population. How are men going to be challenged to grow beyond their narrow premises without the balanced representation of female perspectives to bring inclusivity and insight?

Now for those of you who are trying to wrap your head around the concept of a nonpolitical pro-life position, I invite you to walk in the shoes of a Catholic pacifist. I reject for myself the sanctioned rationalization of the "just war theory" and of the Crusades and of whatever holy wars that countries waged upon each other with God's "blessing" on both sides. This is a point of personal conscience I cannot then apply to everyone else in the world as to how "Christian" they are. I have lived my whole life in a society that is comfortable with the rationalization that training to kill others and Christianity are not incompatible. I will not compromise my conscience, nor will I naively push for a political solution to a deeply rooted spiritual impasse. As long as church leaders along all denominations, "nondenoms," as well are willing to pastor themselves on their flocks by means of significant financial support through political/militaristic/patriotic "theology," they will have abandoned any ability to carry the mantle of a prophetic voice as they remain mired in a lukewarm churchy existence.

The social justice premise I discern from is based upon the needs of the *anawim* (those who have no standing or voice in society, the powerless). In the Old Testament, the anawim, those who are bowed down, were identified as the widow, the orphan, the poor, the incarcerated, and the foreigner. A broader understanding would be the vulnerable, the marginalized, and the socioeconomically oppressed. Advocacy for the migrant comes from the same place as advocacy on behalf of the unborn. Defending the rights of children who lack sustenance, health care, safe communities, and educational opportunities comes from the same place as supporting women in their struggle to be heard and valued. This point of advocacy is quite personal as a lifestyle wherein my mother, my wife, my daughter, and my granddaughters are defended, supported, and listened to and whose aspirations are impressed upon my heart so that I may grow and learn.

Though I have a specific moral premise regarding the rights of the unborn child, it is not for me a black-and-white, task-oriented, issue-focused political platform but a call to conversion and compassion for each individual woman faced with the painful decision of ending the life of an unborn child for so many different reasons, pressures, and forces that leave her with a sense of powerlessness and the illusion that claiming power over her body at the expense of another is justice. The call to compassionate, nonjudgmental relationship with every individual woman in crisis is my responsibility—is our responsibility. How am I to enter the suffering of a mother who bears in her body a child society does not value yet she is expected to value—how unless I and others without political agendas are willing to enter relationship with her?

This level of commitment is several realities removed from the raised voices and the cardboard placards of either pro-choice or pro-life demonstrations. It calls us to value real people over ideology and identity politics. The challenge to enter this level of support and compassion for women who have been thrust into a cycle of powerlessness by our enlightened society would exist if *Roe v. Wade* remains, if it is reversed, or if it never happened at all. I have no stomach for the pharisaical pro-lifers who put a burden on expectant mothers yet do not lift a finger to provide for both the born and unborn children, the voiceless anawim. Antiabortion ≠ pro-life! I also believe that future generations will judge us harshly as they look back with disbelief. "They used to do *what* to their unborn children?" Pro-choice ≠ prowoman.

The sad reality is that so much attention has been given to the procedure of abortion and its political implications that it seems we cannot see the forest for the trees. According to CDC statistics, reported cases of gonorrhea have gone up 29.7 percent among young women and up 46.7 percent in young men. This seems to indicate that in spite of all the political haranguing from both the left and the right on the issue of sex education, young people are more sexually active and/or not using condoms. These statistics would seem unrelated to the abortion issue if not for the fact that the US birthrate has declined for four years in a row and the abortion rate is at nearly a fifty-year low. It would be easy to suspect that pharmaceutical means of ending a pregnancy have increased significantly and will increase in the future with no reliable means of accessing statistical data on its prevalence. To add insult to injury, according to some statistics, only Japan has a higher cost than the United States for childbirth where on average in the US it costs $10,808 with a C-section running around $16,000. If you bundle that with the exorbitant cost of adoption in this country and the dearth of affordable and safe child care, it would seem that the concept of children is highly valued yet children themselves are not valued much at all, born or not.

EIGHT

A CHICKEN IN EVERY POT AND A GUN IN EVERY HAND

A well-regulated militia, being necessary to the
security of a free state, the right of the people to
keep and bear arms, shall not be infringed.

AMENDMENT 2

W ell, that's as clear as mud, unless you are entrenched in
the over two-hundred-year-old quandary of perspective of the
Founding Fathers: federalism versus antifederalism. From here
one launches into the world of individual rights, states' rights, and
the power or lack thereof of the federal government. My sense is
that the Second Amendment was crystal clear to the Founding
Fathers. At any rate, what the "true" intent and meaning were
does not seem to be particularly relevant to the partisans on both
sides of the current gun debate.

Not unlike the pro-choice/pro-life conundrum we are in, the
most extreme language of murder, fear, and impending death
emanates from both sides. The extreme positions cannot allow

for any compromise according to the representative mindsets. The time-honored tradition of not trusting and/or fearing the government has been a thread of continuity since the framing of the bill of rights on the gun rights side of the fence.

This novice's understanding of the historical concept of the right to bear arms hearkens back to the Greeks and later the Romans who saw the bearing of arms as essential to citizenship and for the self-defense of the individual and the defense against tyranny. The more direct historical connection for the American colonists was England's own struggles against the king and the king's abuse of power in the colonies. Though different criteria for bearing arms were applied over the centuries in England—only landowners, only Catholics, only Protestants, etc.—there were two overriding concerns that carried over to the colonies. The first was the raising and keeping of a standing army, a tool of royal oppression that was held in great contempt. The second was the connection between the bearing of arms and the required participation in a local militia. At any rate, the colonists owned guns and besides being a tool for feeding the family and defending one's home in the absence of law enforcement, ownership of a gun allowed for the American Revolution to take place at all.

Battles like King's Hill and the First Saratoga demonstrated that farmers and settlers equipped with civilian hunting rifles could contend with and sometimes defeat trained soldiers armed with military muskets. Fighting for the right to own a military musket would be completely out of historical context though. They owned their personal weapons for food and self-defense and many were required to be a member of their colony's militia.

For those stuck in the either/or paradigm where the Second Amendment is only about bearing arms as part of a state militia or it is only about the absolute right of individuals to own guns, the challenge is to reach beyond one's cultural biases and to get unstuck from the binary dead end. The premise reflection would reveal that there are very basic differences in understanding how to read the Constitution. The appreciation of historical context might allow for some on either side of the argument to embrace a both/and interpretation, which is probably more accurate and definitely more fluid than an either/or position.

An examination of how contemporary thought and experience have been utilized to reinterpret the spirit of the Constitution and still remain faithful to it reveals many important examples of growth and transition. The Fourteenth Amendment addresses the "right to vote," but the only ones referred to as having this right were male inhabitants of a state, at least twenty-one years of age, who are citizens of the United States. Since Black men were not accorded citizenship until the Fourteenth Amendment was passed, it was understood that they could not vote until that right was defined in the Fifteenth Amendment. Women would have to wait for the right to vote until the Nineteenth Amendment was passed some fifty-two years later.

Slavery was negotiated and side-stepped between the North and the South until it tore the country in two with the Civil War. What was allowed was no longer to be tolerated. Term limits for holding the office of president were not seen as necessary until the ratification of the Twenty-second Amendment in 1951. Finally, as sacred as the First Amendment is regarding free speech, defamation, slander, and libel are not protected by it. The First Amendment of the Bill of Rights is not absolute. To promote the unyielding position that any constitutional right is not open to further and evolving interpretation is without merit.

One foundational context is the militia itself. A common

understanding of the term *militia* was held by federalists and anti-federalists alike and it was threefold.

1. The militia existed instead of a standing army to resist foreign aggression.
2. The militia functioned as an internal police force for the states.
3. The militia existed to defend against the use of a federal standing army against the states. On this point, there existed a divergence between the two factions. The federalists interpreted this as a precaution in the unlikely event that the federal government would act with force against a state. The anti-federalists viewed this third point as a necessity in the very likely eventuality that the federal government would use force against a state.

The "minutemen," the name derived from the fact that they could drop what they were doing and respond armed and ready within a minute's time, composed many a militia in the colonies. The romantically famous ride of Paul Revere was a direct response to an attempt by the British to disarm the colonists and to confiscate stockpiled guns and ammunition. The British attempt to disarm the colonists was the fuse to ignite the American Revolution. This attempt also exemplified the greatest fears of the anti-federalists in their not trusting the fledgling national government. This coupled with the idea that the term *army,* as in standing army, referred to mercenaries and did not cast a positive light on any armed force other than the militia.

Many would argue that because we now have law enforcement agencies at every level of government as well as the national guard in each state that these entities fulfill the previous responsibilities of the concept of a militia. Some would go farther and say that because there is no longer a need to form a militia, the right to bear arms is somehow null and void. On the other end of the spectrum are those who engender a generational fear and mistrust of the government not too dissimilar from the anti-federalists. Though our standing army has now taken a place of honor in the American psyche and is no longer something to scorn, federal agencies such as the FBI have now become the targets of hatred and mistrust in the eyes of those involved in the constitutional militia movement. This fundamental mistrust of the federal government is at the heart of the gun debate in this country. Groups, such as the Oath Keepers and the Patriot movement, combine antigovernment rhetoric with their interpretation of the Second Amendment to further expand fear and mistrust of the government among gun owners.

In spite of the very real differences in conclusions drawn in establishing a premise based upon one's interpretation of the Second Amendment, the more basic common challenge is in overcoming mistrust of the other. Gun rights advocates need to ask themselves if they really align themselves philosophically with fringe militia groups against the government and therefore against the vast majority of its citizens who believe in our system of government even with its flaws. Gun control advocates need to ask themselves about their judgments of law-abiding gun owners in the advocacy of stricter gun regulations.

Working toward building trust of fellow Americans who have a different perspective is not all that difficult. If gun control advocates could only appreciate the very real concern gun rights advocates have for our children in public schools, who for so many reasons are as vulnerable as sitting ducks in their classrooms. The concern is authentic though politicized by many. If gun rights advocates could only appreciate that a longer-term perspective and millions of statistics on gun fatalities in our country are why gun control advocates, from their perspective, view the idea of increasing guns on campus to protect the kids is akin to throwing lit matches on a powder keg in the name of keeping the keg from blowing up. What both sides need to ask themselves is "What if those were my kids?" "What if those were my grandkids?" "Will my rhetoric and political philosophy be enough to save them when some crazy, who shouldn't have a gun in his hands in the first place, opens fire on yet another campus?"

Premise and Perspective

I am not, nor will I ever be, a gun owner. I choose not to live in fear pondering what-if scenarios as I believe that I cannot claim to walk in faith when I am really walking in fear. I believe that living in that kind of fear not only affects the way I think by coloring the way I perceive the world but also affects the person I become and affects those around me as well, especially my children and grandchildren. I don't hunt, and I am not inclined to start now. I am part of the over 68 percent of Americans who do not own a gun. I don't get gun ownership like I don't get piercings and tattoos, don't get rap music or death metal, and don't get addiction to social media. It is not part of my culture so I don't get it. The fact is I don't have to get it. Life on earth does not depend on my "getting it" or sharing the same perspectives of everyone around me. The challenge to respect and appreciate those who have different perspectives, opinions, and experiences from me and not making them the "other" is a central key to spiritual growth and discernment if I am humble enough to embrace it. What I don't get at all, and what really does scare me, is that only 3 percent of Americans own half of the 265 million guns out there.

My trust for the average gun owner is neither here nor there. I hope they have more than adequate firearm safety training and I have some concern for their kids, but I don't mistrust them as a whole. I have a good brother in the church who loves to hunt and comes back with photos and stories that turn my stomach, but I have no right to judge him. I keep my opinions to myself and let bygones be bygones. On the other hand, I am very untrusting of some members of that 3 percent who will do anything to impose their version of freedom on my family and me at any cost or loss of life. Sacrificing the lives of innocent kids in poor neighborhoods and on school campuses in the name of their cause is about as un-American as it gets as far as I'm concerned.

What broadens my very narrow perspective are life experiences that I couldn't anticipate. My family had the honor of living in Arkansas for five years. Needless to say, it was a major culture shock for us when our kids came home from school with gun permit applications that were handed out as a matter of course for hunting season. I was freaked out to say the least. The most relevant point to be made is that these weren't hotheads and weirdoes who owned guns. They were just everyday folks who grew up around guns and hunting and it wasn't that big a deal. We, on the other hand, didn't even let our kids play with toy guns when they were growing up. Whatever stereotypes I had about gun owners was blown out of the water. I also remember a piece that I think *60 Minutes* did on gun ownership as they interviewed a family of gun owners and the gun safety training of their kids and the heavy emphasis upon using a gun responsibly. Aside from not relating with these parents on the issue of guns, I related with them on just about everything else. They were real parents with discipline and consistency in their household, and their kids were respectful and quite mature. I related to a gun-owning family on family priorities and on how to raise one's children. This was very refreshing for me, having been a teacher where encountering real parenting was harder and harder to come by.

I can see the Promised Land because I can feel the common ground between those who have a very different perspective and me. We all want what is best for our kids. We all want them to be safe in all environments and at all socioeconomic levels. The common ground can give us the wings to get off of the tit for tat single dimension and respond with compassion and honesty. It isn't an issue of compromise as much as it is an issue of shared vision and working toward a common goal. This is how second-dimensional conversations can start.

The task at hand is to directly call out those who would divide us for their own profit and advancement. I don't trust the NRA because I believe that the expensive lobbying efforts of such organizations have contributed to the erosion of our democratic process such that even if the perception that candidates for office are bought and paid for was not true, the perception is still corrosive to the process. When 67 percent of Americans agree on anything nowadays, such as increased gun control, it would seem nearly miraculous, but that agreement does not turn into policy. This makes little if any sense until you explore how elected officials vote coupled with who contributed to their campaigns. My problem with the NRA—and Big Pharma, the pro-Israel lobby, Big Oil, the tech industry, etc.—is that they are focused on manipulating lawmakers into representing their very narrow interests and not the interests of voting constituents or the American people in general.

The trust issue is very important to me as well in trying to identify and distinguish between my thinking and my feelings of mistrust. A major contrast to my feelings about the NRA is that I trust implicitly my friends who own guns. They are for the most part just salt of the earth folks where trust is not an issue. They are on both sides of the political tightrope, and that isn't even relevant. What is relevant is that they are real people, not internet trolls. They are flesh and blood brothers and sisters whom I don't fear. They are not online and on-the-ground vigilante extremists, whom I fear very much.

I have no problem with acknowledging that gun ownership is a basic right of American citizens and that it is protected by the Constitution. What I have a problem with is the manipulation of historical interpretation in the expansion of gun rights for the sake of increased profits and in the crafting of fear aimed at legitimate gun owners. What I am referring to specifically is propaganda intended for the proliferation of assault rifles and other military arms as if this was our historical heritage.

Two hundred and fifty years ago, no hunter in his right mind would have insisted on or demanded the right to own military muskets over their more accurate hunting rifles. That "right" would have seemed absurd. When the Gatling gun was introduced during the Civil War in the 1860s, you did not have political entities or lobbies pushing toward what would have been seen as a ridiculous demand for the right of private citizens to own their own Gatling gun. Though the cost of the Thompson submachine gun, introduced in 1918, was the most prohibitive factor against very many civilians being able to afford one, there was not some major philosophical argument using constitutional language to promote the proliferation of its use among civilians. Even though organized crime created one of the most violent eras in our history through the use of the Tommy gun, there was no great outcry or political leveraging to promote its use by civilians. Believe it or not, the old NRA used to work with the federal government to limit gun trafficking where it applied to mental patients and ex-convicts.

If NRA advocates really understood and believed the foundational basis for the Second Amendment, then they would be in the front lines of the Black Lives Matter movement. They would understand that militaristic governmental force at any level of government, used against unarmed citizens, strikes at the heart of the Second Amendment because the greatest concern had nothing to do with private ownership of guns as much as it did the ability to organize and defend against a militaristically abusive government. This is precisely why the posse comitatus act restricts the military from engaging in law enforcement on American soil. Once again, those concerns have been addressed as we are no longer afraid to have a standing army and we have several law enforcement agencies at the federal, state, and local levels whose members put their lives on the line for us every day.

So in a nutshell, the thinking of those who were chronologically closer to the origins of what went into the foundational interpretation of the Second Amendment is not consistent with the current politicization advanced by the NRA today. This is a basic premise question as developed in chapter 3. Essentially, all gun owners of good will need to do their own research of the NRA and not take mine or anybody else's research at face value. How did an organization initially dedicated to the promotion of marksmanship transition into becoming a narrowly focused lobbying force? Do your own research on the Institute for Legislative Action and the influence of Harlon Carter. Even if the NRA does not survive its current bankruptcy, the damage of distorting and expanding what gun rights advocacy has become continues to poison public discourse.

If we reflect on the suffering of families who have endured loss as a result of uncontrolled gun access on the streets, in their schools, and in houses of worship, we come to the common and fundamental question time and again: what if it was my kids?

We come to the realization that it can't happen again because all our kids have the right to live—to *just live!* We would see that we need to work together not to punish gun owners and not to allow obstructionist extremists to monopolize the conversation as they ignore the will of the majority of Americans for their own self-absorbed interests.

"We the People" owe it to our kids and to children yet born to find real solutions that aren't steeped in rhetoric and pig-headed one-liners. The convoluted logic represented by the phrase "Guns don't kill people ..." is a coward's way of deflecting the reality that the next school, church, theater, workplace, or concert shooting, and every one after, is on us. We and our refusal to even try to find real solutions are all judged as guilty.

NINE

THE DEATH OF REASON: THE EITHER/OR TRAP AND OTHER FALSE DICHOTOMIES

Have you ever noticed how some fundamentalist Christians are completely dismissive of science as a matter of course? Have you ever noticed how some scientists go out of their way to promote atheism? It would seem that the framework to dismiss "the other" is baked into their respective mindsets, though I doubt either side would admit it.

Have you ever noticed the disdain for moderate Democrats that is espoused by "progressive" Democrats such as Alexandria Ocasio-Cortez? Not unlike the race baiting of the Trump administration, the need for the extreme positions and polarized, monolithic loyalty on either the right or the left creates the either/or false dichotomy of us versus them. Do any of these factions have any experience in consensus building, or is adversarial interaction the one-trick pony they bring to the social/political arena?

This binary conundrum does not allow for shades of gray or layers of nuance. It instead locks people's minds into a black-and-white, single-dimensional world of inflammatory soundbites and rabble chants. I don't have to think if an oversimplified explanation of all that is wrong with the world syncs up with my engrained biases. Show me the preacher or politician who tickles my ears and stokes my fears, and I will show you herds of nonthinking, noncritical, nondiscerning cultists.

So many very good people on the right and on the left are so fearful of not belonging to the herd that they turn a blind eye to the flaws of their positions, their leaders, and more importantly, their worldviews. The lack of both desire and effort to change and grow or repent, as it were, on one's part sets the stage for the lack of critical accountability we have of the political parties and their leaders. Real critical consciousness is self-evaluative in nature as part and parcel of critiquing external systems. As it stands now, the desire for discernment is not a priority and is not even on the list for that matter. Single-issue driven success is all that matters, no matter the cost to the country. Lockstep loyalty to "us" allows for no questioning, no evaluating, and no discerning. To enforce this binary existence, one confronts the herd at great expense. Just ask Representative Justin Amash from Michigan or former Senator Jeff Flake from Arizona about how holding to their convictions is not a trait that was well received by their party or electorate.

So how and why does the death of reason take place in our society? It is not my intention to insult any readers, but have you ever tried watching "reality" tv? It's like the *National Enquirer* on steroids with the brain-massaging effects of video on its side. Suffice it to say that there have to be tens of millions of viewers of this genre; otherwise, the networks wouldn't spend the money they do promoting this form of "entertainment." Just as the rabble in Rome was enthralled with "the games," the new Circus

Maximus is not only the big business of sports entertainment but is now also inclusive of the "reality tv" experience. What better way to turn off one's mind at the end of the day? What better way for the word *reality* to end up meaning absolutely nothing in these staged for TV spectacles? I am also convinced that HBO has a "gratuitous sex and violence" desk that ensures that there is enough frontal nudity and blood to make the cut.

Another opportunity for the death of reason is found in the practice of seeking out and associating with like-minded people. This occurs in where we choose to live, work, worship, and especially online. If we all like each other's narrow-minded posts, then it stands to an absence of reason that we must all be right. If my small mindedness is never challenged, then there is no need to learn and grow and question my reality. Such are the echo chambers that allow for "War is peace. Freedom is slavery. Ignorance is strength," going back to Orwell's classic, *1984*. The main difference is that I freely participate in my own brainwashing by failing to utilize my brain at all. I submit to the conditioning of my choice and blindly follow the next Pied Piper who comes along playing my preconditioned melody preference. Just as in the passage of time where the year 1984 has come and gone without much fanfare, perhaps the lack of true awareness of our motivations and impulses, which depend on external prompting, has become a "reality" that also went unnoticed— that by design went unnoticed. *1984* did in fact come and go unnoticed.

Even though the word *rationalization* comes from the Latin words *ratio* and *rationis,* which mean reason, account, prudence, etc., it doesn't mean that the only function of reason is to justify my positions or biases. Reason can also be a part of critical discernment. The relevant critique is not revealed in the inconsistencies or specks in the eye of the "other" but is revealed in questions like "What if I am wrong?" and "What if I don't care if I am wrong?" It is also revealed in the knowledge that my position is in error because I have chosen to deceive others or that even though I am wrong, I won't back down on my position no matter what the consequences are. In these examples, true discernment is either helped or rejected by either the humility I choose to embrace about myself and my capacity to be absolutely wrong or by the pride and arrogance that poison my soul, where deception and a lack of remorse for how others are affected do not trouble my self-serving "reasoning."

Referring to the premise exercise from chapter 3, some recurring premises for wrongheadedness and justification are "The ends justify the means," "America: love it or leave it," "American interests are paramount," and manifest destiny. Any one of those well-intended premises can lay the foundation for the perception of a greater good or nobler cause where concepts, such as wrong, immoral, or unethical, are easily dismissed in the name of something seemingly much more profound. If I can never get to the place where I admit to the flaws of my cherished premises, then I will not discern right from wrong or good from bad—or even care at all.

From a merely intellectual perspective, a flawed premise undermines any conclusions that follow. From a Christian perspective, I would have to quote Jesus's response to the Pharisees. "If you were blind, you would have no sin; but now you are saying 'We see.' So your sin remains" (John 9:41 NAB). This goes to the heart of self-righteousness. While I am waiting for the rest of the world to come over to how I think and what I believe, I am incapable of admitting fault or error of any kind. I am incapable of remorse. I cannot repent because I do not perceive any need for repentance.

This lack of repentance is essential and is foundational to

the culture of intolerance that the whole world is manifesting. Intolerance assists us in boiling our prejudices into political and emotional ammunition against those we hold responsible for all that is wrong with the world. Intolerance provides us with the means to scapegoat a race, religion, or culture that is just too foreign for me to accept as my intolerance defines me. I am now ripe for being manipulated by politicians, fearmongers, Russians, or any one of my online "friends" who have drunk from the same "Kool-Aid" recipe of intolerance.

At this point, my "truth" is so false and my blindness is so absolute that real facts, as opposed to "alternative facts," have no impact on my reasoning at all. It is the others who are deluded. When my go-to response hearkens to "fake news" or the "deep state," I can't discern the truth because I don't really want to know the truth. Nothing diminishes the process of discernment more than the conscious decision to not discern at all. From Twitter pronouncements to Facebook conspiracy theories, the internet has only served to accelerate to instantaneousness of Mark Twain's comment "A lie can travel halfway round the world while the truth is putting on its shoes." It is by our active participation in digitally disseminating divisive Russian propaganda that we all have the wonderful opportunity to become Russian operatives.

> President Putin and the Russian security services operate like a super PAC. They deploy millions of dollars to weaponize our own political opposition research and false narratives. When we are consumed by partisan rancor, we cannot combat these external forces as they seek to divide us against each other, degrade our institutions, and destroy the faith of the American people in our

democracy. (Dr. Fiona Hill's opening statement
of her testimony in the impeachment hearings
before the House Intelligence Committee,
November 21, 2019)

Intolerance is often the identifying characteristic of
fundamentalism, which often gets a bum rap representing
narrow-mindedness or reactionary thinking, but it doesn't
have to be that way. In sports, having the fundamentals down
is essential. My dad, a coach, had me making left-handed layups
for hours along with free throws and other solitary activities. As
a musician and teacher, I have students practicing scales and/
or rudiments so that their technical facility will give them the
freedom to make music.

Fundamentals boil things down to basic components and
essential qualities that can then be easily taught and built upon.
The problem with some "fundamentalists" is the belief that their
way is the only way and that the need to define and delineate a
black-and-white version of what to believe and how to live—a
black-and-white version of reality, if you will—inherently brings
with it division, accusation, and condemnation of "the others."
It is often misconstrued that fundamentalism is an exclusively
conservative characteristic, but progressive liberals just as easily
fall into black-and-white myopia. This can be easily illustrated
when political factions call for issue X to be a litmus test for true
believers. As a result, the two dominant political parties are for
the most part intolerant of divergent views. Pro-life Democrats
are looked down upon with scorn by the party leadership.
Republicans who speak out against Trump in the name of
decency and Republican ideals risk losing support from the party
poo-bahs. This intolerance drives potential candidates to either
capitulate or to not run at all. It also drives the issues without any

substantive dialogue or debate. More importantly, the populace as a whole tends to accept the predigested platforms or more precisely propaganda of the left and the right.

Thinking is not required as so many people are prone to believe according to their biases and not according to the facts. Think of the sports analogy once again as to whether or not player X was out of bounds. Not even super slo-mo replay of the Mueller report will change any interpretations because people's minds were already made up before it was read. More precisely, I would hazard to guess that most of the population did not read any part of the documents because their minds were already made up.

The irony of it all is that the same personality traits and needs for black-and-white interpretations of reality and distinction are the same in al-Qaida as in white nationalists. They are the same in antifa as in neo-Nazis. They are the same in the desire to impose Sharia law as demanding prayer in schools. ISIS and the Westboro Baptist Church are merely opposite sides of the same coin of intolerance. What is feared most by both the extreme right and the extreme left are true pluralism, real cultural diversity, and authentic ethnic inclusivity. The left gives intellectual lip service to the theoretical ideal of diversity just as long as it isn't authentic independent thought that does not tow the party line. The right makes no bones about its worship of nationalism and the enthroning of xenophobia as a lawful purpose and has become intolerant of dissenting opinions among the rank-and-file Republicans. Thus, fundamentalism demands adherence and not creative thinking—all at the expense of real discernment.

The long-lost cousin of fundamentalism is relativism. Once again, it was thought that relativism was solely the child of free-thinking liberals and situational ethicists of the 1960s, but it has found a home among science-denying conservatives as well as among some nondenominational Christians who now seem to have a sliding morality standard for Trump that didn't exist at all for Clinton. The reason for bringing up relativism is that any place of honor that "truth" had in ages past has long since been abandoned for the slick and easy soundbites designed for the indiscriminate consumer of prepackaged media.

To illustrate an example of extreme relativism, no matter where someone is on the political spectrum, I would imagine that most of us reacted in the same way upon hearing about Rachel Dolezal. She was the White woman who worked her way up the ranks of the NAACP in Washington state under the guise of being Black. It seems that she really believed that she was not White but was in fact African American. She sold it, and people fell for it because she believed it. The objective truth of the situation was relegated to a place of irrelevance and her self-delusion got her all the way to the role of president of the NAACP in Spokane, Washington. The operative term here is *self-delusion.*

Relativism wedded with fundamentalism is a dangerous pair to contend with. On the one hand, you have a black-and-white worldview that ostracizes infidels, and on the other hand, truth is up for grabs and can be manufactured with the latest tweet or campaign smear with the reality TV crowd eating it all up without question. Throw on top of that a disdain for legitimate news organizations as "fake news," and you end up with a populace filled with doubt and mistrust for the government, business, education, religion, media, and any form of idealism. Without the anchor of at least mutual trust, all that is left is fear.

Premise and Perspective

I will not pretend to be an opinionless person who lives in a world of moderate bliss. This just isn't so, yet I can't be easily catalogued either. One-dimensional thinkers cannot allow for the possibility of leaving the tightrope of polarizing extremes and of going beyond the ease of binary codification. Most of us realize that real life is full of gray areas, yet when it comes to partisan loyalties, we adhere to our tribal folklore with a vengeance. No matter how far beyond our comfort zones we navigate away from familiar shores in our daily interactions, we often fail to bring that same resiliency to the ideological realm of black and white.

I can easily be labeled a "social conservative," yet I personally have a difficult time relating with self-identified social conservatives. I will expand upon my position that only by abandoning one-dimensional polarization and by allowing our ideas to reach second- and third-dimensional perspectives can we truly dialogue in mutual respect for each other. I will use an expanded version of the premise identifying process from chapter 3 to illustrate my thinking on the immigration issues we are confronted with presently. In this process, I hope that it will become obvious that as hard as one tries, attempting to pigeonhole my positions and opinions on a single line is not possible. I am really lazy about how daunting the task of accurately illustrating my thinking may be and preoccupied about how exhaustively I want to endeavor in this effort, so I hope I don't cut any corners in the process.

The two dominant premises that inform my thinking on any and all immigration issues are sacred scripture and Catholic social teaching. An objective study of history and some understanding of the Constitution and immigration law are also foundational for me. The Old Testament references on how to treat the alien or the foreigner are numerous and crystal clear. Christ's teachings at the sermon on the mount, the Good Samaritan, Matthew 25:31–46, the women at the well, etc. are also very clear. St. Paul's teaching in Galatians and Colossians about the breaking down of distinctions couldn't be any clearer. These are just a summary of the relevant scriptures. The fact that Mary and Joseph were on a forced journey to Bethlehem for a census imposed by an occupying force and were later refugees fleeing terroristic killings after Jesus was born speaks volumes to the current plight of refugees.

I have the honor of encountering unaccompanied minors from Central and South America every week as part of the RICO ministry of our parish. In this ministry, I come face-to-face with Jesus Christ as a child and have the awesome opportunity to serve Him in these children. I also spent time assisting in the care of immigrants through other ministries in the church.

Living on the US-Mexico border has also left me with both contradictory and biased perceptions, and when combined with my upbringing, they are quite cold and stark. As stated in chapter 6, my father was born in Mexico. He lived for several years in a state of limbo in his attempts to become a US citizen and would have been in very similar circumstances as today's "Dreamers." He was a very proud man and would never consider receiving government assistance of any kind. Having been raised in this environment, my wife and I couldn't think of applying for welfare even though both of us worked and were still below the poverty line in our early years of marriage. We did take advantage of WIC when the children were infants and there was no money left in the bank to feed them. We also sent our kids to school with sack lunches like we used to do when we were kids and witnessed a great many families on the free lunch program or on food stamps who drove late-model cars and wore the latest fashions while we did our best to keep our clunkers running and clothe our children in hand-me-downs. Just like the stereotypes, we saw many welfare mommas who kept having kids to keep the checks coming and also those who were masters of playing the system through fraud and loopholes.

To add insult to injury, the last years of my father's life were spent in declining health with ever-mounting medical bills for my mother to contend with and the revelation that my dad's employment at Safeway when he was a young man must have been off the books due to his undocumented status, so his Social Security contributions and consequently payments were affected in his declining years through the deception of his then manager. Even though my dad worked hard all his life, became a US citizen, built up retirement savings, and kept his insurance policies up to date, my mom still had to liquidate all their assets apart from selling their house so as to not go completely broke due to medical bills resulting from a prolonged illness. How can a self-made man who went through the pitfalls and labyrinths of attaining citizenship put himself and his wife through college while working at least two jobs at a time and did everything according to the "American dream" end up with only a house over his wife's head when he died? Balance this very real family experience with the fact that undocumented individuals who have never paid into the system can receive free medical care under our current system. And don't get me started on full-term young women who come across the border on the verge of delivering a child for the sole purpose of taking advantage of the Fourteenth Amendment provision for attaining citizenship for their child. I understand it, but I don't like it one bit. This also applies to the Chinese and Russian travel mechanisms that generate top dollar by arranging for the prize of a US birth. US citizenship for sale, anyone?

I also carry prejudiced attitudes toward erratic Mexican drivers without any form of insurance, arrogant Mexican shoppers, and as a former teacher in Catholic schools, toward some upper-middle-class Mexican families who failed to teach their children about respect for others. Do you have me figured out yet?

The absolutely most ridiculous presupposition I have absorbed in my assimilation process is the misguided notion that as a native-born American, my life is somehow more valuable or meaningful than that of an immigrant. It is as if to say that as an American citizen, I am part of God's chosen people somehow. The conclusions drawn through cultural osmosis are that I have more claim to human rights. I am somehow more deserving of respect and my human dignity is a foregone conclusion but immigrants have hoops to jump through to earn any rights, any respect, and any value of them as persons with innate, God-given dignity. This is why the adjectives *illegal* and *undocumented* just roll off the tongue when attached to the words *immigrant* or *alien*. The concept of "the rule of law" creates a comfortable distinction between me and those people.

Of course, on an intellectual level, on a conscious level, I don't believe any of that, but that doesn't mitigate the effects of the nativism that lives just below skin level on the fringe of my psyche. It's as if to say, "What value is there in being a member of the American 'us' if I can't conjure up some abstraction of fringe benefits denied to the non-American 'them'?" I have a full privilege membership card to the human race, thank you.

I love history, not grade school propaganda but the real thing from original sources. This is why MAGA makes little if any sense to me. From my reading of US history, so much of our supposed "greatness" was a result of the sins for which no repentance is forthcoming, namely slavery, genocide, expansionism, and capitalism. I believe that unless a nation's sense of greatness is shared equally among all its citizens, then it is merely the romantic musings of the conquering culture.

Slavery altered the lives of thousands of Black Africans and later, native-born descendants and made the ruling class both in the North and the South very wealthy. Slavery also had deep roots in the young nation with systemic racism poisoning all its institutions. The symptoms of this poison are just as lethal today for African Americans as in the days of the Greenwood Massacre of 1921 in Tulsa and the legacy of the Shubuta Bridge in Mississippi. How can we make any claim to greatness when so many Americans still believe that they are racially superior to others and indoctrinate their children with this same poison?

The national disgrace of our treatment of Native Americans and the genocide of whole nations or peoples should have our heads bowed from now until eternity. I wonder how those who use the buzz phrase "the rule of law" apply that to the over five hundred treaties that have been broken by our government. This doesn't even count the treaties that were signed under false pretense by individuals who were not recognized tribal signatories. Full disclosure, on October 12, 1992, I observed the International Day of Solidarity and Mourning with Indigenous Peoples of the Americas by dressing our three children, then ages seven, four, and one, in red sweat bottoms and tops that I customized with as many indigenous iron-on symbols from as many nations and regions as I could find and sent the older two to school that way. I instructed my boys, the older two, to respond to questions about their "Indian" designs with the fact that Columbus was lost and made a mistake by referring to the people he encountered as "Indios." He wasn't in India as he thought, so we shouldn't repeat Columbus's mistake. We should know better. Our daughter Sarah, the one-year-old, just looked cute without any historical coaching. Needless to say, I have a very strong opinion on this ongoing tragedy.

I wonder how many members of "the party of Lincoln" know that the then-Whig US Representative from Illinois, Abraham Lincoln, challenged the validity of waging the war against Mexico. Lincoln introduced the "Spot Resolutions" that challenged President James K. Polk, a Democrat, to submit evidence that the initial cause and the first battle of the war was fought on American territory. History shows that Polk created the conflict and that the reason for starting the war was under the false pretense that Americans were killed in combat on American soil when in fact the first battle took place along the border with Texas, which at the time was not part of the United States. Mexico lost about one-third of its territory as a direct result of US expansionism. To this day, we still reap the profits of having waged and won an unjust war against Mexico. Once again, that same tired phrase about the "rule of law" is the justification for inhumane treatment of refugees from Central America when the true rule of law was abandoned at the outset and resulted in an unlawful war and in the resetting of the border with Mexico.

In summation, the Darwinian nature of capitalism was foundational to the historical realities of slavery, genocide, and expansionism as it created a dynamic whereby some people prospered on the backs and lives of other human beings. With the pseudoreligious propaganda of manifest destiny on its side, all real moral considerations were settled without the need for any real discernment. The indigenous peoples and the country of Mexico were simply obstacles to God's plan. Essentially, if one believes that God is in your corner, everything you do is right and just and in His name, so what is there to discern? The term *American interests* is used to this day to justify questionable actions on the part of the US government.

So how does someone with seemingly contradictory experiences, biases, and foundational premise philosophies extrapolate any manageable perspective or guiding principles without serious discernment? Well first, I need to honestly look at my strong feelings and biases, especially the ones where I harbor resentment or anger. First of all, I am American born and raised, but I will never be American or "White enough" for a certain segment of the population. My cultural heritage is from Mexico, but as an assimilated "Americano," I will never be Mexican enough for even my relatives back in Mexico. I have no need or desire to be identified as Hispanic, Latino, Chicano, Mexican American, and especially Latinx. It's bad enough that others require that I be put into an identity prison, so why would I do the same thing to myself or to anyone else?

I don't have any personal interests in bringing over relatives into the United States, which would more than skew my objectivity, nor do I fall for the fear-laden propaganda of how inherently dangerous undocumented immigrants are to our national security. I live on the border. The contrast between the violence in Ciudad Juarez and that of El Paso are like night and day. It was not that many years ago that the weekly murder rate in Juarez was higher than almost any place in the world. There were maybe two degrees of separation between most El Pasoans and victims in Juarez. I will always remember a young student from Juarez who, after the Christmas holidays, came back to school so sad and reclusive. I pulled her aside and asked what was wrong. Through tears, she told me that her grandfather, a shopkeeper in Juarez, was extorted to pay protection money to one of the gangs. He refused and was gunned down on Christmas Day in broad daylight.

Though the murder rate in El Paso is quite low for a city its size, El Paso has not been impervious to terror and mass shootings. On August 3, 2019, on an unremarkable Saturday morning at Walmart, our collective experience in El Paso of that same level of violence came as a result of homegrown white nationalism and not from immigrants.

Most of us would agree that our current immigration policy is severely flawed at best. What many of us don't realize is that US immigration law has been the weapon of choice in legislating racist policies to combat the possible immigration of undesirables. The Naturalization Act of 1790 limited naturalization to "free white persons of good character." The Page Act of 1875 banned Chinese women from immigrating into the United States. The Chinese Exclusion Act of 1882 prohibited all immigration of Chinese laborers. Between 1917 and 1924, laws were passed restricting certain kinds of immigrants, such as the Asian Exclusion Act and the National Origins Act. The Immigration Act of 1917 barred those who were physically or mentally ill and excluded southern and eastern Europeans, most Asians, Africans, and Arabs, and those who could not read or write. When the ideal of American hegemony was threatened, the US passed the Emergency Quota Act of 1921 and later the Immigration Act of 1924 limiting the immigration of particular groups and nationalities.

It has been suggested that during the Great Irish potato famine, the poor Irish Catholic immigrants were turned away from ports in Boston and New York due to anti-Irish, anti-Catholic sentiment and were redirected to the Port of New Orleans. An immediate consequence of this redirection was the death of thousands of Irish Catholic immigrants who contracted cholera, yellow fever, and/or malaria. Incidentally, the potato famine ran from 1846 to 1851. The founding of the anti-Catholic

Know Nothing Party was right in the middle of that time period in 1849.

To better understand the racism inherent in American thought, one only has to look at the response to Japanese Americans after the bombing of Pearl Harbor. Through Executive Order 9066, over 115,000 US Japanese Americans were "relocated," a euphemism for having property seized combined with unlawful arrest and internment, even though the vast majority were United States citizens. Both Italian Americans and German Americans experienced some degree of nativist hatred and discrimination yet were similar enough in appearance not to undergo some of the most blatant of racist policies leveraged by the federal government.

I don't believe in open borders. I believe in the sovereign right of a nation to define and enforce its immigration process. I believe that we need just immigration laws and that current law is long outdated. I believe we need to have objective dialogue about the Fourteenth Amendment and whether or not it is time to reconsider birthright citizenship since the issue of incorporating native-born male slaves into the electorate has not been an issue for several generations now. I believe that since we are failing the working poor, the elderly, the homeless, and the millions of families who would be devastated financially should they suffer a major medical event, we need to be very careful not to discriminate against poor citizens in our well-intentioned efforts to serve immigrants and their needs. This becomes even more critical when we realize that there are over six hundred thousand homeless people in America and over one in ten homeless are veterans. It makes me wonder what intrinsic value our citizenship has when so many citizens are devalued. Of course, lack of just and affordable medical and mental health opportunities is at the heart of these issues.

I believe that we as a nation are reaping the fruit of severely flawed Latin American policies where we have supported despots and dictators in the name of American interests that only served to bolster the influence of anti-American socialists and their increasing influence in the region. Instead of pursuing mutually beneficial relationships with Latin American countries where economic growth and democratic principles became the norm, we have taken advantage of certain situations by supporting the ruling class with a blind eye as long as our interests were served.

Last but not least in the cause-and-effect principle at work in our current immigration crisis at our southern borders is the fact that our nation's drug use has torn some countries apart to supply our insatiable hunger for drugs. This is a supply and demand conundrum that has spawned the growth of drug cartels, small time gangs, and corrupt police who terrorize people through extortion, torture, and murder. Refugees from Central America are fleeing the violence we helped to create. We are to blame through our voracious demand for drugs and our failed policies that fostered the maintenance of "banana republics" with little chance for diversification and economic growth. The fact that we failed to adhere to our own laws concerning refugees who are seeking asylum only adds to the tragedy.

There exist no simple solutions as all the above considerations do not neatly fit into an oversimplified, binary political position. As long as politicians from both parties are fixated on appeasing their respective bases, with the oversimplified goals ranging from open borders to building a wall, the real work of solving this crisis in a humane way won't even be attempted. At this point, even though the narrowness of my limited perspective can't provide real solutions to this issue without the consideration of other perspectives, I can provide an imagining of possible second- and third-dimensional frameworks that break from the binary, either/or stalemate.

First, we must address our sense of equity and all that entails. A sense of fairness or parity seems to be fundamental to finding justice in all situations, but I as an American have a particularly skewed perception of fairness because I am a "have" by most standards and not a "have not." How else can I define my sense of distinction and accomplishment? I am male so I have one fewer glass ceiling to break through than my sisters who have to be twice as competent to get 20 percent less pay than their male counterparts. If I were White as well, I would have one more vast layer of entitlement to contend with in my struggle to really arrive at an honest perception of justice.

This honesty about my skewed perception makes me one of the blind men who encounter the elephant so it therefore demands that I incorporate the views of women, of the "have nots," and of immigrants, but am I willing to hear their stories?

My anger and frustration regarding my dad's final years and about how the social welfare system, which I believe is gamed so that honest work is not rewarded and dishonest representation is both rewarded and encouraged as an almost generational inheritance, needs voice, but not at the expense of scapegoating immigrants. Even as a pacifist, it is alarming for me to encounter so many homeless veterans and our sense of despair over the homeless needs to be heard, but not as a sophistic argument to bolster our xenophobia. The oversimplified summation or conclusion is that if we can't take care of our own, how can we take care of all these immigrants?

Without blindly promoting solutions to the aforementioned issues, informed by a desire to adjust for my learned prejudices, I would like to endeavor to stand common issues on their heads and get to the possible root causes of these situations. From my perspective, without honestly addressing these possible causes, any political positions or solutions are without much merit, no matter how well intentioned they are.

Earlier, I mentioned in passing that affordable medical and mental health opportunities are at the heart of these issues. This in the same way that the cost of childbirth in our country has to have an impact on a woman's discernment about even having a child at all. If this is so, then no political position from socialized medicine to the Affordable Care Act to maintaining the status quo is ever going to solve the problems. I believe that the problem simply lies in the blind and unquestioning acceptance of for-profit health care. There are so many people making so much money in the medical, insurance, and pharmaceutical sectors, with the promise of so much financial reward, that we have reached a moral impasse. For-profit health care is the way the system is set up, and throwing money at it—money from employers, insurance companies, the government, and regular people—is like throwing money into a black hole. As has been suggested by others about the design of such systems, it isn't a question of fixing a broken health care system because the system is functioning exactly as it was designed. We need to retool the way we think about the physical and mental health of all our citizens and what it is costing us not only in money but in moral decay, self-respect, and human dignity. As long as health care is about respective parties getting their piece of the overpriced pie, or their pound of flesh as it were, every attempt at fixing the problem will never be more than a Band-Aid. NYU has chosen to offer a full-tuition scholarship to all students in its MD program. This is a fundamental step in the right direction as reducing the debt of those who have chosen to become doctors is foundational to reducing overall medical costs.

Now before I go much further, you might be wondering how

far this tangent goes before it returns to the issue if immigration. What I am trying to illustrate is that our failure to care for all our citizens in a just and compassionate fashion breeds an attitude of exclusivity or entitlement and is only exacerbated when applied to "foreigners," which is not that inexplicable when viewed from a "charity begins at home" perspective. The seeming impossibility of making a course correction in how we do health care only enhances the fear that there are not enough resources and not enough money to go around as it is so we can't take care of immigrants if we can't take care of ourselves. The whole reason for cracking the lid ajar on the Pandora's box of health care is to illustrate that my sense of entitlement allows me to distance myself from those who are different from me by completely denying that I am connected to them at all. This disconnection from the others is at the core of nationalism where the rhetoric of "the rule of law" gets repurposed to fit the level of and justification for disconnection.

This is where my own reflection as a Catholic and upon Catholic social teaching runs in direct opposition to my sense of entitlement and my desire to distinguish myself from immigrants so as to maintain the illusion of disconnection from foreigners, those somehow less deserving of dignity, those who somehow do not merit all that is afforded me in my Americanness. If I am to remain Catholic, I must embrace that within the unity of Eucharist there are no borders and there is no entitlement other than the grace of God given freely to all. Whatever fears I foster in my uniquely American brand of Christianity, I cannot hold on to as a means of justifying my anger about what my dad went through, my anger about those who use the system, and my decision to avoid and deflect any sense of connectedness to immigrants and still be authentically Catholic.

Even the well-intentioned realization of "There but for the

grace of God go I" is grounded in one's distinction from and not solidarity with the homeless, the junkies, the poor, and the immigrants or whatever poor unfortunate one comes across. How else can one forget where they came from? How else can someone remain ignorant of the hatred and struggle that their grandparents and great-grandparents endured upon coming to America? Not only must I confront my tribal tendency to distinguish between us and them, but I must also come face-to-face with my self-defining, capitalistic demand that I am either a have or a have-not. Only after I have discarded the illusion of my idealized self can I acknowledge the sin of my own self-absorption which revels in the distorted goal of "I got mine." Only after I have engaged in honest self-examination of the reasons behind my biases and opinions as part of an authentic attempt to realize that my perspective is only one of many will I be capable of entering honest dialogue with other people of good will who consider the welfare of people over agendas and ideology.

In closing this chapter, I would posit that the only thing real about the concept of "my reality" is that it is based on my very real reference point. My acceptance of the truth that only my reference point is real and that all my conclusions are based upon a reference point might help me to accept the possibility that I may be functioning from a false premise, and it might also help me to not take myself so seriously as reflected in the following joke.

A man feared his wife wasn't hearing as well as she used to and he thought she might need a hearing aid. Not quite sure how to approach her, he called the family doctor to discuss the problem. The doctor told him there was a simple, informal test the husband could perform to give the doctor a better idea of her hearing loss.

"Here's what you do," said the doctor. "Stand about fifteen feet away from her and speak in a normal conversational tone to see if she hears you. If she doesn't hear you, move to ten feet away, then five feet away, and so on until you get a response."

That evening, the wife was in the kitchen cooking dinner, and her husband was in the den. He thought, *I'm about fifteen feet away. Let's see what happens.*

Then in a normal tone, he asked, "Honey, what's for dinner?" No response.

So the husband moved closer to the kitchen, about ten feet from his wife, and repeated, "Honey, what's for dinner?" Still no response.

Next, he moved into the dining room where, he was about five feet from his wife, and asked, "Honey, what's for dinner?" Again, no response. So he walked up to the kitchen door, about three feet away. "Honey, what's for dinner?"

Again, there was no response. So he walked right up behind her. "Honey, what's for dinner?"

"Ralph, for the *fifth* time, it's chicken."

TEN

THE POLITICS OF SEXUALITY

There is neither Jew nor Greek, there is neither
slave nor free person, there is not male and
female; for you are all one in Christ Jesus.

GALATIANS 3:28

I realize that quoting the Bible might put some people off just as a matter of principle, but there is method in the madness in an attempt to explore or examine the disconnect between using sexuality as a means of power and oppression and the myriad of ideals that exist as they attempt to redefine sexuality and gender roles in a more just fashion. There is no better example of missing the mark and human imperfection than is exemplified in the beautiful words of St. Paul cast against his insistence that wives be obedient to their husbands and that women should have their heads covered as well as not speak in public gatherings, as he teaches in 1 Corinthians. Paul's insistence that slaves be obedient to their masters was fodder for "Christian" slave owners of all denominations to continue to justify the sin of slavery. How can one individual be so close to a unifying vision of discarding meaningless distinctions yet so way off in application?

Though it would only be too easy to superimpose one's "enlightened" twenty-first-century sensibilities and judgments onto a man who lived in a completely different cultural and historical world than we do, the real task is to apply the realization of the existence of such a disconnect in one's own thinking and relationships in spite of how enlightened one imagines them self to be. My potential for self-delusion in the area of the politics of sexuality cannot be separated from my very narrow perspective of my own sexuality. Even if I am politically engaged with like-minded individuals either on the "right" or the "left," and my narrow perspective is reinforced by the strength of numbers, this does not preclude the possibility that I and my like-minded cohorts just all happen to be grasping the legs of the elephant and are therefore convinced that the elephant is in fact most like a tree. This narrowness of perspective applies equally to the members of the Westboro Baptist Church on the right as it does to those on the left who have used "outing" as a justified political weapon. It applies equally to those who called the AIDS epidemic a "punishment from God" as it does to those who retooled the term *homophobic* to mean anyone who has any reservations about any aspect of the LGBTQ political agenda.

Now those on the extreme left or right might take exception to being compared to "those people," but I would maintain that myopia exists across the spectrum and serves the function of filtering data for those whose minds are already made up. We don't dialogue. We shout and scream. We don't search for answers about something as basic and natural as our own sexuality. What we do is go through our own journeys in silence, in private, and then we join the tribe that has drawn the most similar conclusions—even if they are entirely wrong. So many of us use Kinsey as evidence of real data and draw the conclusions we maintained beforehand instead of understanding that Kinsey was a very good snapshot of a time, a culture, and a nation living in the midst of sexual repression, but that is it. The same can be said of the work of Masters and Johnson in that we are provided with a time capsule of data about sexuality. They are a beginning but are not, nor will they ever be, an end-all-be-all revelation, questions answered, book slammed shut!

So essentially, I am returning to the image of the blind men and the elephant full force because our "absolute" opinions have very real and very devastating consequences, and as a result, we value ideology over people time and time again. Those with the most extreme positions won't even come up for air long enough to see the damage they inflict. So how do people change and view others with differing perspectives as brothers and sisters and not as the enemy? This is a core question that is not being asked in the body politic on issues of sexuality or anything else for that matter.

Let us examine some specific examples dealing with premise, response/lack of response, personal beliefs, and how they affect both the national conversation and political policy. This exercise is a tool to identify our less-than-ideal collective responses to the needs of others based upon some very flawed premises in the area of sexuality. The following paragraphs are intended to be snippets of our common experience that help us to ask authentic questions in search of unknown answers, as opposed to parroting predigested rhetoric through confirmation bias filters.

Once again, let us consider a significant health issue that affected the whole nation but was not perceived and responded to in either a timely or compassionate manner. Of course, I am referring to the AIDS epidemic. In Africa, even though it was understood to be a sexually transmitted disease, it was a disease that crossed all demographics and entire populations. It was a health crisis, period. In the United States in the early eighties, it was viewed as an issue that affected gay men. The fact that African Americans and Hispanics were disproportionately affected by AIDS did not help the situation.

Each of us who was living during that time has a unique recording, if you will, of how AIDS and people infected with AIDS were reacted to in society. These questions remain: Would our response as a nation have been different if AIDS had been viewed as a national health crisis and not as a gay men's disease? What if prominent preachers with national audiences had not preached that AIDS was a punishment from God in wrathful judgment of gays? What if very well-meaning politicians who would have gladly allocated funds and awareness for a health crisis but not for something that looks like a gay issue had gotten involved? Would it have taken heroes, such as Ryan White and Princess Diana, and celebrities like Elton John to challenge us to snap out of our sexual/political indifference?

On another issue, what does "being a man" mean? What is a man allowed to do and not allowed to do psychologically and emotionally? Now ramp your answer up significantly and ask the same question within the context of a military community. Our national struggle with the question of toxic masculinity and macho expectations has always been amplified for men serving in the military. Most of us know that the suicide rate among veterans is very high compared to the general population, but do most realize that estimates from between 321 and 541 active-duty members of the military took their lives in 2018? It has only been in the last few years that the military has taken a different approach in dealing with soldiers under psychological stress and has now opened some doors to treatment as opposed to routine discharge as in the past.

Perhaps coincidentally, even as so many police departments run their academies like pseudo boot camps to weed out the weaklings, so to speak, not only to determine physical stamina but to denigrate and subjugate the potential candidates, the suicide rate for law enforcement officers has been significantly higher than the rate of those who have died in the line of duty for three years in a row. The question remains about where the political will is to not only examine these issues closely but to reexamine what it means to be a man in our culture? What level of male toxicity will we tolerate in both political and social discourse? What will we teach our sons about what it means to be a man? Do we bring up soldiers and law enforcement officers when it is time to wave flags, march in parades, and make political hay and then just as quickly put them on a back shelf, "out of sight, out of mind"?

This begs the question of what we will teach our daughters about what it means to be a woman. Two songs come to mind to reveal such stark realities and observations. The first is "It's a Man's World" by James Brown, and the second is "Woman Is the Nigger of the World" by John Lennon. I encourage the reader to do a search on the lyrics and then decide if this is the reality you want your daughter to accept without question. The irony is that neither musician had a glowing reputation about their treatment of women, though it can be said that Lennon reprioritized his values and ultimately became a better husband and father, but I digress.

Do little girls really believe that they can one day be president in a country that still has failed to elect a female president? More to the point, would you vote for a woman candidate for president of the United States? Are there still those who would not vote for a woman just because she is a woman? If not, why not? For those of you who say you would vote for a woman, what "male" qualities does she need to possess for you to even consider voting for her? As this hypothetical candidate walks on the tightrope of impossible expectations, at what point does she become too shrill for you or too much of a "bitch" for you or exhibit too much attitude for your liking? Does a woman really have to become a "dragon lady" to get her point across? Does a woman need to exhibit strength in exactly the same way that we expect from men?

The politics of business and corporate advancement for women are the same in the political sphere where the innate strength of a woman is measured in how much she emulates classic male behavior. To advance, it would seem that a woman needs to give up her sense of the common welfare and instead look out for number 1. She needs to leave behind compassion and instead demonstrate that she can make hard decisions. She needs to abandon empathy and exhibit arrogance. It's as if a woman had to give up the terrible vulnerability revealed by asking for directions when lost and instead never asked anyone for directions for fear of appearing like not having it all together and of not being completely self-reliant. Sound familiar? I already said that I will never be "White enough" for some people, probably because I am not White. If men fear not appearing man enough, what chance does a woman have?

Imagine a world where we valued women for who they are with strengths and unique insights that are different from those of men. What if women having a place at the table meant that we junked the long board room table of male hierarchy and had round tables instead, or several round tables, or no tables at all? What if women who shared common strengths as men would be viewed as integral and not as threats? What if strong women were valued and cherished instead of feared and denigrated? What if we as a society allowed women to raise the bar of political discourse instead of expecting women to mudsling along with the men? What if women held themselves to a higher standard out of self-respect because they really know better, having endured a lifetime of double standards built upon the most unlevel of playing fields?

On the issue of male hierarchy, how can it be possible that the NRA has any interest in the Violence against Women Reauthorization Act of 2019? Without getting bogged down in the intricate details of how this legislation has been tweaked to appease so many concerns, the process seems to have gotten boiled down to a premise contrast once again with the NRA scorecard used as a leveraging tool. The philosophical premises at odds with each other are simply the perceived rights of the individual and the perceived rights of society—in this instance, potential victims. We as a society need to discern whether or not any form of arms restriction for a certain population should automatically be considered a threat to the Second Amendment. Likewise, we need to consider the consequences for an underrepresented population, namely women, who are disproportionately the victims of relationship violence. Not to do so would be as ridiculous as blindly allowing Congress to determine the course of health care for the citizens they represent, even though those same politicians have a separate "sweetheart" health package deal. Can you imagine it?

Now take the same philosophical premises and flip them to opposite political camps when it comes to the subject of abortion. Neither the NRA lobbyist nor the pro-choice activist would be capable of acknowledging that they are intellectual reflections of each other. My perceived rights outweigh all other considerations regardless of the consequences. I redefine reality itself so that it marches in lockstep with my blinders. This is an issue having everything to do with the politics of sexuality not merely because it has been made the hood ornament of a certain version of feminism but because it is the ultimate sweep under the rug, after the fact Band Aid that allows us to avoid the real conversation of the nonvaluing of women in our society and who the masters still are. Did men adopt a female perspective on sexual expression, or did women sell out their sisters in the name of sexual liberation? Girls from childhood through their teenage years have always valued the mystery of relationships whereas boys are raised to see girls as a means to an end, namely ejaculation. This self-serving perspective affects males in all stages of life and forms their worldview. Can we say, "America First"?

The whole issue of unintended pregnancies is the ultimate result of a society that not only allows for but promotes the subjugation of girls and women through sex where misogynists get what they want with few if any consequences and sexually liberated ideologues allow for the psychological manipulation of the desire for a relationship under the guise of a feminist sense of sexual parity. The sad reality about abortion is that we aren't accounting for the missing figures in the societal math. As I stated before, the central crisis of abortion is a spiritual one, but either extreme would have you obediently vote according to presumptions made about political outcomes. The missing figures I refer to is the unknown quantity resulting from pharmaceutical abortions. There has been a steady decline in abortions performed in the last few years. There has also been a steady decline in the birth rate the last few years. Dominant trends in sex education notwithstanding, these figures would seem to reinforce each other if it wasn't for the fact that there has been a steady increase in STDs the last few years. More precisely, we are at epidemic proportions. Check the figures yourself. Do the research. Verify if I am making it all up. Take the initiative and seek out what is true and real because the only explanation for this increase is unprotected sex. So where is the accounting for all those statistical pregnancies from all this unprotected sex coinciding with a decline in the birth rate?

Speaking of a sense of sexual parity, I am reminded of the Grammy Awards of 2018 where women artists from every generation made a musical statement of solidarity as Kesha performed "Praying" drawn from her legal battle with her producer. It was powerful but was ultimately relegated to being a symbol of token political messaging when seen in the light of what actually occurred that evening. The best pop solo performance went to Ed Sheeran, who happened to be the only male nominated against four very talented females. This is neither here nor there except for the fact that "Shape of You" is about a man's search for a hook-up and is yet one more song that objectifies women. "I'm in love with your body." Seriously, in this day and age, that is still a marketable lyric? To top it off, the live performance of "Despacito" was perhaps better suited for a stripper bar. Sex still sells, and as long as the culture both serves and eats it up, all these high-minded ideals about the dignity and value of women beyond sex amounts to just more industry hypocrisy attempting to appear responsive in this era of "Me To" and "Time's Up." The male-dominated recording industry giving up its misogynistic investments yet appearing responsive to women's issues is akin to the fossil fuel industry expanding into clean energy—only if the cash keeps flowing.

Now regarding "Me Too" and "Time's Up," these movements are as long overdue as examination of rape kits across the nation, in some cases for as long as decades. With this said, we must still thoughtfully consider the social dynamic of pendulums in cultural dynamics. What do these two movements and the Innocence Project have in common? They deal with victims who are ignored and dismissed by a broken social justice system and are thus further victimized. On one hand, female victims of violence and sexual abuse are not taken seriously. Their word has little if any value. On the other hand, we have not yet transitioned away from men of color being falsely accused and being sent up the river without any semblance of justice being attempted. If we lose balance as a result of the swinging pendulum, then we are all perpetrators.

The issues surrounding LGBTQ rights is a conundrum all on its own. I don't fully understand the artificial grouping of these different communities other than the social phenomenon that they are all catching the same wave of personal realities and resistance to hypocritical religion that the rest of society is riding at the moment, kind of like a class action, societal pariah opportunity. The difficulty in attempting real dialogue has shifted from not only having to deal with sexuality Nazis on the right but the sexuality Nazis on the left as well. The real victims are children who have to sift through all our absoluteness. What if the whole concept of inborn sexual identity is a myth? What if the imposition of societal gender roles is in fact destructive? (Toxic masculinity.) What if adults are projecting their false conclusions onto kids? Just as sure as children of members of the Westboro Baptist Church are being taught to hate, today's kids run the risk of drawing wrong absolutist conclusions about their sexuality as a result of the prevailing political/sexual climate. Is every person who does not draw the same conclusions as you regarding what constitutes sexual identity automatically the enemy? What happens when one side's version of reality becomes prevailing public policy? How do we as a nation balance between religious rights and sexual identity rights, and are they mutually exclusive?

Premise and Perspective

So how has my journey formed my fundamental beliefs, and how are they similar to or different from the absolute positions that are predominant today? Well first of all, my upbringing as a Catholic is pretty foundational with some exceptions. I believe that the church's hang-ups on the subject of sexuality have been very destructive to the spiritual life of the faithful. It seems that hating one's body is a prerequisite for all the guilt that comes with adolescence. The church's desire to make a positive statement about virginity, with celibacy somehow reflecting the kingdom of heaven, has actually had the reverse effect in communicating how fleshy and sinful the rest of us are. A wonderful exception to this is the work "Theology of the Body" by Pope St. John Paul II.

First of all, both of my parents worked so the radical idea of a woman working outside the home was very natural to me, though not so common in the sixties. The positive outlook I derived from this is that a married couple can be equal partners in providing for the family, which takes the economic and societal pressure off the husband. The struggle to throw off the shackles of role expectations still remained to be worked through as I entered adulthood, but I had already grown accustomed to being a square peg in a round hole in other areas of my life, so this was just another divergence from the norm for me. The downside is that as a child, I longed to spend more time with my parents. They were too busy being providers, which formed my whole notion of what a family could be without dumping all the responsibility on the woman.

As a musician, I have had the wonderful experience of playing "in the pit" for dozens of musicals beginning in high school and have even been onstage for a couple of shows. I was exposed peripherally to "gay" interactions in the theater world and formed many negative opinions about those relationships I witnessed, which had nothing to do with moral judgment on my part and everything to do with an aversion to relationship dysfunction and promiscuous license. Being "come onto" did not help my conclusions in the least. The homosexual casting couches were never discussed yet everyone knew, once roles were ultimately cast. I witnessed boys who went from having a great enthusiasm for theater at the beginning of a run only to become swishing lispers by the end of the run. It's anecdotal at best, I realize, but the whole role-playing characteristics reminded me of "jocks" playing the macho roles through gross and degrading behavior and humor almost always at the expense of someone else. Role-playing is still role-playing no matter how effeminate or how macho one believes they have to be. If it were not for the many friends I made in theater, I would not have many positive experiences to draw from at all regarding homosexuality.

In short, since there is not as yet any scientific evidence of a homosexual gene, and as a student of history knowing that the Spartans nurtured young boys to engage in strong homosexual bonding as soldiers, I don't believe that people are born with any particular sexual orientation at all. With this said, does it therefore follow that I am automatically the enemy for some and I am just a hater at heart? Allow me to continue. There are friends I love who are like members of the family who identify as gay and live accordingly. I have very many professional relationships from years in the music scene who are homosexual in lifestyle. My approval of their lifestyles is not a prerequisite for my loving them deeply.

But probably the most profound experience I had on the issue of gay culture in our society and upon my psyche was being at the deathbed of a young man dying of AIDS. It was in the early to mid-1980s when I was a parish youth minster and when there was so much ignorance and fear concerning AIDS. A priest friend came by my office at the parish and asked me to be a signer on a will for this young man. He explained the situation to me, and I already knew that I wasn't going to catch AIDS by being in the same room with the young man, though the average ignorant American would have advised me against it. Father Tony explained to me how this young man's prominent Catholic family had rejected him and wanted nothing to do with such a sinner who brought great shame to the family. I believe they even told him he was going to hell.

I was around twenty-three or four at the time and he was just a few years older than me, though you wouldn't know that from his emaciated appearance. Now my focus was on his needs and I had to, with great effort, keep my focus on him for this was my first exposure to an extremely gay environment. Many of his friends were there, which I should have anticipated as totally natural, but when we were greeted at the door by a "nellie" with a T-shirt that read in bold letters, "TUNA YECCH, BUNS MMM," I was freaked out to my core and tried to maintain my absolute best poker face. The posters inside the house were sexually graphic, and I found myself trying not to look either left or right and not raising my eyes. His friends were gathered around the bed in such sadness but with so much love and support. He was so grateful with a gentle kindness in his eyes, and we held hands and prayed before Father Tony and I left.

I was confronted with my personal leper, as it were, in the form of this frail young man. I was confronted and came up wanting. Yes, I responded when needed, but it was almost an intellectual exercise in doing the right thing but lacking in compassion and true love.

Soon after this time, our first child, Anthony, was born. Father Steve, the pastor in the parish I worked in, allowed me to shift my schedule to evenings and weekends so that I could be the primary caretaker for Anthony during the day when Karen worked. Up to today, being a "househusband" was the most difficult job I have ever done or will ever do. I was psychologically and emotionally ill equipped for the task. I dealt with bouts of low self-esteem and frustration that I had thought were beneath me, and even my idealistic liberated male constructs could not avail me from what I imagined women had endured for generations. Fortunately, times have changed and more men are inclined to share in all aspects of creating and maintaining a loving home through the sharing of all responsibilities that make a nurturing family possible. What a martyr I was.

So how do I maintain any sense of balance when it comes to dealing with seemingly oppositional positions within myself when viewed through the lens of current political polarization on topics of gender and sexuality? First of all, my journey has instilled in me that the struggle between dehumanization and politicization is central in both forming my interior disposition as well as whether or not I encounter others with compassion or with judgment. Discernment proceeds from this journey. I am hyper suspect of political agendas and propaganda from all sides with all the sophistries they promote to engage their self-righteous base of acolytes.

What forms my central core in the area of civil rights for those who live homosexual lifestyles is the tragedy of Matthew Shepard. Even though I maintain my beliefs about sexual orientation, to not be crushed and changed by the murder of this young man and to not call out the hatred that was at the black heart of his torture and murder is to align myself with the evil hatred that to this day permeates every level of our society. With this said, I stand just as firmly against so much of the LGBTQ political and cultural agenda as I do the Westboro Baptist church or the so-called Christian "Faggots are Maggots" tour of Mike Heath. There is no moderate view in dealing with either hatred or with self-serving distortions of reality. Again, this isn't an exercise in finding a middle ground but an exercise in abandoning the futile thinking in one dimension, which only leads to polarization.

This is where it is essential to fully understand one's premises, be they objectively correct or not, so as to follow each premise through to its logical outcome or to realize that one's premise is not only flawed but is inconsistent with what a person really believes and holds to be true. The failure or inability of an individual to either consistently build upon or discard a premise is part of the explanation for cognitive dissonance or hypocrisy in less charitable terms, where one is not willing to change one's behavior or flawed reasoning, usually to serve perceived self-interests. The reason I bring this up is that a core premise for me is the concept of free will. I totally reject any form of predestination-based explanations either religious or en vogue "I was born this way" social trends in thought. The corollary to this of course is that I bear the full responsibility for my actions. I can't blame my past or my wounds or my genes for my choices. I will not cut myself slack for my mistakes. I alone am responsible.

Even though religious predestination is as far right on the spectrum as you can go, promotion of sexual orientation as genetic and inevitable, a left-leaning belief, is merely the opposite side of the same, identical coin. The results are the same. Dialogue is impossible because the case is closed. People are artificially grouped into castes by those in power and are taught to live out the self-fulfilling prophecy of their role in society. Free will and human potential are abandoned because of the ardent desire to settle any questions, to arrive at closure, and as a result, "to settle" for self-serving answers. This well intentioned religious or ideological fervor results in the conditioning of the masses with the most vulnerable victims being children and teenagers. Children try on many hats on the journey to becoming. If one-third of college students end up changing their major, why is there such an urgent political push for children to be saddled with a socially influenced sexual identity or orientation for life?

I believe that the real problem is the absurdity of our societal gender roles and expectations. As weirded out as I am by nonbinary kids, I stand in absolute admiration for how bravely they refuse to jump through anyone's hoops. All the role-playing is suspect—all the roles. The agendas to force machismo on boys and prissiness on girls are as oppressive as many of the LGBTQ agendas to force their perception of reality on the rest of us. Human potential is so much greater than predigested conclusions on human behavior. The mind is so much more subtle and complex than quick-fix "ergos" to human sexuality can allow for. If you think what works for you works for you, great, but why foist it on anyone else?

One particular basis for my point of view has to do with counseling teenagers primarily during the seventies and eighties and helping them deal with sexual issues where they were overwhelmed with guilt, low self-esteem, and thoughts of committing suicide, which were all derived from forgone conclusions about same-sex experimentation and rejection from society, their families, and the church. The pendulum was way off-kilter toward rejection, but at least there was the possibility of working toward self-acceptance without the imposition of any forgone conclusions. Having a same-sex encounter meant nothing more than the fact that it happened and working through whatever issues the individual may have been burdened by. Openly discussing issues associated with arousal and intimacy and how that is all a part of growing up removed the stigma without putting the kid in a box. I don't know if that kind of discussion can happen nowadays because the pendulum is now at the other extreme and parents support their five-year-olds in arriving at "conclusions" about their sexual orientation or identity. To "conclude," by definition, shuts all other doors.

In all this, my main concern is the problem of polarized thinking itself, which will not allow for shades of gray or real dialogue. Remember that fundamentalists or puritans for that matter are intolerant of other positions and they exist on the left and the right. To illustrate what I mean, I will go back to my passing reference to the word *homophobic* and its retooling as part of the LGBTQ strategy to force issues by labeling all who have different perspectives as haters. I remember a time when homophobic meant ignorant and fearful of homosexuals where misinformed individuals relied on stereotypes. Many times, homophobic concepts influenced public policy, such as fearing that teachers who identified as homosexuals would automatically be child molesters when there has never been any study to indicate that this is true. This is simple ignorance, but it isn't hatred.

Most people can differentiate between sexism and misogyny. In terms of the political interests regarding same-sex relationships, any effort to identify distinct attitudes and issues is discarded in favor of a push toward an all-or-nothing—dare I say fundamentalistic—view of the world where only black and white exist. This means that the thugs who beat up "fags" are the same as legislators who believe that allowing for same-sex marriages will adversely affect the institution of marriage are the same as the baker who will not make cakes for same-sex weddings out of religious principles. It is politically expedient to artificially group them together under the banner of "haters" so as to force the issue that all manner of legislation representative of same-sex interests is somehow intrinsically just and any opposition is automatically hateful and despicable and therefore unjust. Such polarizing techniques have been used over and over again by the NRA and the Trump administration, except that this maneuvering comes from the left.

A critical analysis and comparison of each scenario reveals completely different motivations and interests of the aforementioned individuals. Just like all other hate groups, those who seek to physically harm others with different sexual lifestyles from their own operate out of pure hatred and loathing and to some degree an irrational fear of those who are different. Their position is one of complete intolerance. The legislators who are attempting to represent their constituents in favor of the "traditional" family make ignorant and by my standards homophobic arguments about saving the institution of marriage when in fact heterosexual couples have already done a good job of wrecking the whole concept of marriage all by themselves, thank you. The individual who can't in conscience prepare a cake for a same-sex marriage for religious reasons is coming from a completely different place from the previous two examples. Such an expression of one's faith is also completely different from refusing to allow entrance to one's bakery or refusing to sell one's prepared wares that are readily available to the general public, which would in fact be discrimination. There is absolutely nothing automatically hateful or discriminatory about someone who has a different perspective on what marriage is. What is lacking is dialogue. When policy is made in the absence of creative dialogue, the result will be polarization not only as a result of opposing views but because of a sense that a segment of the population feels ignored and therefore irrelevant to the conversation. This political arrogance cuts both ways just as the pendulum of popular opinion has nothing to do with justice.

Examples for comparison would be the trend toward the legalization of marijuana usage in some states. What if a law came from the federal government that defined an individual's constitutional rights to smoke weed? What if by federal mandate all prostitution was no longer illegal, as in several counties in Nevada? Now overnight, societal norms have to artificially adjust to the new standards. Everyone with a dissenting view would be ostracized for getting an intellectual whiplash and for not sheepishly going along with it.

The classic failed example from our own history is the success of the Anti-Saloon League, an entity closely affiliated with Protestant evangelicals, to finally push the passage of the Eighteenth Amendment to the Constitution. So how is legislating morality that different from legislating ideology, especially when a large segment of society is scorned for not being in lockstep with the prevailing winds of trending views? As is predictable in a money-centered society such as our own, just as the national income tax of 1913 helped to set the stage for the Volstead Act, replacing revenue from liquor sales, the Great Depression laid the groundwork for its repeal. The high-minded moral arguments were not as relevant with as much as a 60 percent reduction of income tax revenue in just a few years.

This is where I return to the whole idea of dehumanization and/or demonization of one's "opponent." It is when I value ideology over people that I pigeonhole their reality on my terms, whether or not I claim to be progressive or conservative. The tendency to view my fellow American as an opponent at all is at the heart of the matter. If I feel a need to quench my righteous thirst with the swill of divisive media, then all discernment has ceased. This is not intended to reference the "them" of one's scorn as much as it is a measure for self-reflection. Where the rubber meets the road regarding my sexual/societal conditioning as a human being is whether I value competition over cooperation, winning over consensus, power over serving, arrogance over humility, and class/racial distinction over unity.

The most fundamental form of politics of any kind is language, and this is sadly the case in the politics of sexuality from the most conservative to the most liberal. Just as presented in chapter 2, "Words Matter," I would encourage everyone to ask themselves if they use words of violence, denigration, and dominance by saying, "What a pussy," "He's such a dick," "Fucked up," "Got screwed" "My junk," "Top or bottom?" and on and on. Our sexual terminology reeks of oppression and belittles the gift of procreation and intimacy. Our words betray how corrupted and alienated we have become from our own bodies and from each other. Unlike less advanced cultures, we seem to have forgotten that breasts are for the nourishment of infants and not for the promotion of a trillion-dollar skin industry rooted in oppression and human trafficking. This alienation from each other can only be challenged by a deep longing for unity and a welcoming of true diversity and not just "think like me" left-leaning versions of diversity.

The ability or even just the willingness to seek unity in diversity instead of inevitable polar opposition is at the heart of jumping onto a second and even third dimension of vision where shades of gray give way to many colors of possibilities. In closing on this topic of the politics of sexuality, I offer you a quote from a woman in Iowa who wanted her caucus voting card returned after finding out that Pete Buttigieg was married to a man. "Then I don't want anyone like that in the White House." As sad as that statement is, I am even more dismayed by angry gay rights advocates who do not think that Mayor Pete is "gay enough" when it comes to "gay" issues. Are you kidding me?

For those who have decided to put me in the "haters" box because of my views on sexual orientation, I believe that Mayor Pete was the best candidate for the presidency of the United States, but wouldn't you know that it came down to two old White guys left among the Democrats to run against another old White guy in November. *Are you kidding me?*

ELEVEN

THE SEPARATION OF CHURCH AND STATE AND SWALLOWING A CAMEL

Congress shall make no law respecting an
establishment of religion, or prohibiting the
free exercise thereof; or abridging the freedom
of speech, or of the press; or the right of the
people peaceably to assemble, and to petition
the Government for a redress of grievances.

AMENDMENT 1

Separation of church and state is a concept based in the Establishment Clause, found in the First Amendment of the US Constitution. The Establishment Clause prohibits the creation of legislation addressing the establishment of religion. Think in terms of state-sponsored religion.

The term "separation of church and state" does not appear in the amendment itself or anywhere else in the Constitution. This does not mean that the meaning behind the term was not fully understood. We often use our common understanding of our constitutional rights to discuss our clearly defined right to privacy or right to a fair trial and in this context, our right to religious liberty, though none of those terms appear in the Constitution either. We debate the use of assault rifles by private citizens in reference to the Second Amendment, even though they did not exist when it was written.

The idea of the separation of church and state can be traced to William Penn, who was persecuted in England for being a Quaker and subsequently founded Pennsylvania, to John Clarke who was persecuted in Massachusetts for being a Baptist and was a cofounder of Rhode Island, and of course to Roger Williams.

To go back to the probable origin of the term "separation of church and state," it is generally believed to have originated in a letter from Thomas Jefferson to the Danbury Baptist Church dated January 1, 1802.

> Believing with you that religion is a matter which lies solely between man and his God, that he owes account to none other for his faith or his worship, that the legislative powers of government reach actions only, and not opinions, I contemplate with sovereign reverence that act of the whole American people which declared that their legislature should "make no law respecting an establishment of religion, or prohibiting the free exercise thereof," *thus building a wall of separation between church and State.* Adhering to this expression of the supreme will of the nation in behalf of the rights of conscience, I shall see with sincere satisfaction the progress of those sentiments which tend to restore to man all his

natural rights, convinced he has no natural right
in opposition to his social duties.

Even though an apparent contradiction in thinking or
tension exists between application of the Establishment Clause
and the Free Exercise Clause, which protects religious freedom,
it would seem that English history itself and the framers' own
quest for religious freedom clearly established that one freedom
was built upon the other or that one freedom could not exist
without the other. In the Establishment Clause, no state-
sponsored religion would infringe upon the free expression
of each citizen's religious beliefs. Current controversial issues
pertaining to the Establishment Clause involve religious symbols
in public displays and school prayer as well as federal funding of
private religious schools, among others. Controversial issues
pertaining to the Free Exercise Clause include the right of a cake
maker to refuse to bake wedding cakes for same-sex weddings
and sex education in public schools or mandating that anyone
should be bound by a law that goes against one's conscience
or religious teaching. One might argue that the whole idea of
teaching or not teaching creationism in public schools straddles
both clauses as creationists demand that the biblical version of
creation be taught alongside evolution in public schools while
others maintain that the teaching of creationism in a public
school is tantamount to establishing a state-sponsored religion.

As if to directly address the European abuses of religious
favoritism in the holding of political office, the framers also gave
us Article Six to level the playing field, so to speak.

Article Six of the United States Constitution establishes
the laws and treaties of the United States made in accordance
with it as the supreme law of the land, forbids a religious test
as a requirement for holding a governmental position, and

holds the United States under the Constitution responsible for debts incurred by the United States under the Articles of Confederation.

> The Senators and Representatives before mentioned, and the Members of the several State Legislatures, and all executive and judicial Officers, both of the United States and of the several States, shall be bound by Oath or Affirmation, to support this Constitution; but no religious Test shall ever be required as a Qualification to any Office or public Trust under the United States. (Article Six)

As we look into the experience of sectarian violence and persecution in Europe as well as the influence of John Locke on how human rights were perceived and of the baron of Montesquieu who gave us the idea of the separation of powers in government, it is not a mystery what the intentions of the framers of the Constitution meant in both Article Six and Amendment 1 of the Constitution. Many of the problems we face today concerning the relationship between religion and government seem to stem from exclusive emphasis upon either the Establishment Clause or upon the Free Exercise Clause as if they were not joined in the same sentence. I would also posit that the partisan rancor and power struggles we see in the nomination process of justices to the Supreme Court are in fact a violation of Article Six by both political parties, but I'll address that later.

So how do we learn to dialogue objectively and constructively about the many impasses we encounter regarding the relationship between church and state, especially in a culture where we are advised to never discuss politics and religion, and here we have a blending of both?

Perhaps one common shared experience where we can start is revealed in the extreme emotions that are drawn upon and up to now have served to divide us to the extreme. I am referring to the unusually visceral emotion each of us experiences when we perceive that someone is attempting to "shove something down my throat!" The response is almost immediate, but more importantly, it is a universal response. This experience is common among atheists as well as Orthodox Jews, common between humanists and Latin-only Catholics. So how is it that we forget our anger and the sense of indignity and the overwhelming feelings of oppression when we then turn around and impose our views on others politically, culturally, or legislatively? Why do we feel so free to dump on others in ways that we would never tolerate ourselves? I would suggest that we examine our own history of the dehumanization of others and politicization of our own beliefs to the detriment of others.

The ideals put forth in Amendment 1 are just that: ideals that we have not ever fully realized. Without having to spend any time referring to the blood of religious persecution spilled in Europe, we have our own "we should have known better" examples to reflect on. How is it that people who were searching for religious freedom could devalue Native American culture, beliefs, and humanity so easily? Not coincidentally, the new arrivals to this continent had a very strong sense of their personal rights being fleshed out in land ownership and also in being chosen by God to come to this new land, not that differently from the tribes of Israel assuming ownership over the "promised land." The sacredness of the land and the ebb and flow of nature and human relationship to the land and its animals was never a consideration. The social politics of colonizing and expansion and concepts of personal rights and religious freedom applied only to one race but not the other. My purpose is not to judge the pilgrims but to illustrate how we continue to be oblivious to others in the establishing of a universe where our perceived rights are paramount over the rights of others.

Puritans who were persecuted in England turned around and persecuted Baptists in Massachusetts. Catholics in Maryland who had fled persecution from the Anglican Church passed the Maryland Toleration Act, which allowed freedom of worship for all Trinitarian Christians but called for anyone who denied the divinity of Jesus to be put to death. Our track record on religious tolerance has been hit and miss since the beginning. After the Revolutionary War and the ratification of the US Constitution, perhaps the most notable example of religious persecution was that toward members of the Church of Jesus Christ of Latter-day Saints. Having fled New York state and then Ohio, they encountered severe conflict in Missouri, which escalated at the Battle of Crooked River in 1838 during the Missouri Mormon War. Now Missouri had been a state since 1821 and you would think was bound by the principles of the US Constitution, but this did not keep Governor Liburn Boggs from creating Missouri Executive Order 44, otherwise known as the "Extermination Order," whereby the Mormons were to be treated as enemies and exterminated or driven from the state. The most recent anti-Mormon intolerance was displayed in 2012 when many evangelical Christians spoke publicly against then Republican presidential candidate Mitt Romney because he is Mormon, not unlike the anti-Catholic sentiment that JFK faced in his bid for the presidency.

So how do we work together to better realize the ideals proposed in the First Amendment? Perhaps we need to always consider that our perceived rights must always be considered against the rights of others, be they in the majority or in the minority of the population, and that advocating any legislation having any possible effect on religious freedom be openly and creatively dialogued upon so as to develop a deeper understanding of how people will be affected. Through this process, headstrong special interests would be immediately suspect since the body politic would become less adversarial and more comprehensive and inclusive.

Premise and Perspective

When I went to school in the 1960s, I remember us being given little "red letter" editions of the King James Version of the New Testament. I didn't realize it then as a child, but one version of Christianity was being imposed on me by a government-sponsored and government-funded entity as I was Catholic and our church used a different Bible from the King James Version. I remember the school Christmas pageants and was struck by the fact that Mary was always played by a blonde girl in the nativity scene, but I didn't think much of it then. In retrospect, it was a Eurocentric version of Mary and Jesus that was being imposed on us as well. I can't say that any proselytizing was taking place, but I can say that one very narrow version of Christianity was being promoted over other versions. The obvious issues could have and should have been addressed and resolved locally, but we never got the opportunity as the Supreme Court shut the door on dialogue.

I remember anti-Catholic billboards in West Texas within forty miles or so of where I-20 forks from I-10 and how it seemed that the freedom of speech part of the First Amendment seemed to trump the free exercise of religion part when one's denomination is a minority.

I also have a fond memory of my friend Sam Kirk asking me

to help him at a vacation Bible school at his dad's church during the summer after our eighth grade year, though Father Finnegan would not have approved of my being at a Baptist church. I was so blessed to share in that experience and those little kids who blew this ignorant Catholic out of the water when it came to Bible races. At no risk to my faith, I attended services at other churches as a teenager and played in my first Christian rock band when I was eighteen as drums were not permitted in Catholic churches in the 1970s. Though I was looked down upon when folks found out that I was still a practicing Catholic, for the most part, those naysayers were in the minority.

All these experiences and many others affected how I came to appreciate the freedom of religion and how I became sensitive to what it felt like not to fit in because of my faith. The not fitting in, the feeling that I don't belong or that I am not being heard—these are the insidious or cancerous societal expressions of disenfranchisement that eat away at social cohesiveness and plow the field for extremist responses by those who feel forgotten. This cancer quietly eats away at the fabric of a society as entities jockey for power, influence, and legislation that is to their advantage, but the cancer remains unseen and authentic cures or real solutions are regarded as unobtainable or—even worse—irrelevant.

My honest read of the Establishment Clause and of the Free Exercise Clause is quite broad but not contradictory to the original intent. Since some of the founders were theists at best and not members of mainstream religions and others represented different denominations, it does not seem to me that the issue was ever one of belief in God or any divine entity but was specifically concerned with the potential for influence of a denomination or belief system that might be officially adopted and in a position of influencing the nature of a government based upon its particular philosophical view of life at the expense of the free will and right of the people to follow their own belief systems. No belief system would be allowed to use the government to its own ends and thereby nullify the right of people to believe as they choose. What was given to us was the opportunity to develop a philosophical or ethical pluralism that attempted to consider the rights of the society and of the individual not as mutually exclusive but as symbiotic and therefore integral to ongoing development.

The way this understanding is applied removes the overly narrow characteristic of theistic categories and instead applies the principles of the negative effects of philosophical and cultural influence over a government and its imposition of philosophical and ethical adherence upon the populace. This translates to no ism will be officially sanctioned by and imposed on the governed by the government. Just as the control over affairs of state occurred in the Holy Roman Empire according to medieval societal norms or the Church of England and its monarchy were indistinguishable from each other and thereby persecuted all other denominations, so too would a dominant belief system, promoted by the government against the will of its people, amount to the same outcome and was to be avoided by the writing of the First Amendment.

If it isn't painfully obvious by now where I am going with this, I would like to delineate the progression of isms and how they dovetail but only with specific characteristics common to some but not all of them. The obvious first category would have examples, such as Catholicism, Calvinism, Protestantism, Mormonism, Hinduism, and Islam. They are all religions with a philosophy of life and moral or ethical code. The second category that includes bridging examples would be Eastern philosophies, such as Buddhism or Taoism, that have a spiritual element but are technically not religions but traditionally classified as such and would therefore fall under Amendment 1, although they are not theistic. Though not religions, they also promote a philosophy of life and moral or ethical code. The third category are those that have found a backdoor entrance where they are at present not constrained by Amendment 1 and go by the names of humanism, secularism, nationalism, and atheism, among others. The fourth and last category includes special interest groups or lobbyists who are in fact surrogates for the first three categories as well as those groups that are organized, have a membership, collect funds from their members, and use these funds to promote a belief system or philosophy of life by means of influencing government policy to their advantage.

Now I am not attempting to convince anybody of this huge stretch in thinking as I am not particularly well studied in constitutional law, but I am attempting to illustrate how we have chosen to completely ignore the spirit of Amendment 1 as we strain all variety of gnats and swallow all variety of camels, humps and all. The sad reality is that partisans on both extremes engage in this travesty of justice and disregard for fairness on behalf of their "sacred cow" issues to the detriment of the Constitution itself. Having neither the will nor the skills to dialogue creatively, we allow our self-made polarized culture to form our minds in the reflection of antagonistic confrontation and division at all costs. We don't understand balance. We don't appreciate consensus. We dread the evolution required out of fear of what true diversity and plurality will look like. Those who are attracted to homogeneity and nationalism fear this process the most.

In a step-by step analysis of how the four categories of isms dovetail and are really different expressions of the same subjugation to a dominant belief system, which the framers wanted to avoid at all costs, we will examine each category and its similarities to the others.

Category 1 is the obvious example of where all hell would break lose if any denomination was seen as pulling the strings behind the scenes, as it were, to both its own advantage and for the inculcation of belief and influence of thought over the citizens. It is in this category that we expend most of our attention in order to strain the many variety of gnats we encounter.

In spite of our indisputable Judeo-Christian cultural heritage, we wrangle over nativity scenes on public property and images of the Ten Commandments in court buildings. But we also consider application of the Free Exercise clause in the cake-baking case and whether or not the Little Sisters of the Poor can be forced by federal edict to go against their religious beliefs in the imposition of the "contraceptive mandate." These questions are all worthy of dialogue, but we don't know how to enter covenant with each other so we draw lines and choose sides. We pass laws with a "let the chips fall where they may" kind of attitude. It's almost as if this paradigm demands that people have to be pushed into a "no one is going to shove something down my throat" corner to then allow the machinery of "justice" to kick in. Supreme Court decisions have been made over school prayer, but the matter is far from having been resolved. But again, I digress. The point to emphasize is that we need to be on guard that no particular denomination's beliefs be used by the government to deny or suppress the rights of individuals or minority faith groups. It seems that the First Amendment was not taking on Religion—with a capital R—as much as it was addressing the potential for the unwanted influence of one denomination on matters of state.

Our efforts are both awkward and at times regressive, but the process will take time.

The reason that I refer to the examples of the second

category as "bridging" is because they are not religions at all, yet the same standards can and should be applied to them. As much as I love Buddhist philosophy, I along with the Dalai Lama am heartbroken at how hardline Buddhist monks in Myanmar have exercised influence over government policy in the ethnic cleansing of Rohingya Muslims from the country. The monks are in fact part of a larger hardline nationalist movement that equates Buddhism with the cultural heritage and identity of Myanmar. So yes, proponents of the nonreligion, Buddhism, can both manipulate government policy and persecute members of another faith. Both the Establishment Clause and the Free Exercise Clause of our Constitution would apply to this example if it occurred in the United States—Muslim bands notwithstanding.

By understanding the second category, it has been established that Eastern philosophies, nontheistic entities that are not in fact religions but still promote their own moral or ethical code do in fact come under the application of Amendment 1. It is with this interpretation that a deeper examination of the effects that Western philosophical isms have upon the functioning of government is required.

Since we live in a Western society, there are numerous Western philosophical schools that our culture has been influenced by in its development just as surely as the Enlightenment directly affected our own historical sense of personal rights and self-determination. This sociological integration of various schools of philosophical thought is to be expected in the natural development of cultures and is therefore not the type of sphere of influence that is to be examined. The sphere of influence to focus upon is more akin to the consequences that nationalism and the appropriation of Nietzsche's philosophy of the "Superman," which Hitler leveraged in Nazi Germany, had on the political and social corruption of that country. The politically integrated philosophies of the eugenics of Francis Galton, nationalism, the appropriation of Nietzsche and racial purity, created the atmosphere where the whole moral compass of a country was distorted to the point that atrocities became expressions of patriotism. Wrong became right.

It would seem too easy to cite the horrors of Nazi Germany at making this point, but Adolf Hitler referenced American history to justify Nazism. Hitler admired America's extermination of the Native Americans as what he saw as the superior race expanding its influence according to manifest destiny. Hitler also admired how Americans unashamedly wrote their immigration law to favor northern Europeans by "excluding certain races from naturalization." This control of who was deemed worthy of becoming an American citizen was one of many examples that the United States government legislated according to the principles of eugenics. This same philosophy manifested itself into law by the process of forced sterilization of tens of thousands of Americans who suffered from mental illness and also the forced sterilization of some minorities. American law and lawmakers deemed who was and who wasn't worthy to procreate. Even the United States Supreme Court ruled that forced sterilization of the handicapped does not violate the Constitution in *Buck v. Bell* (274 US 200, 1927). Thirty-three states allowed for involuntary sterilization.

The Virginia statute that the ruling of *Buck v. Bell* supported was designed in part by the eugenicist Harry H. Laughlin. Laughlin saw the need to create a "Model Law" that could withstand a test of constitutional scrutiny, clearing the way for future sterilization operations. Hitler closely modeled his "Law for the Prevention of Hereditarily Diseased Offspring" on Laughlin's "Model Law." At the Nuremberg Trials, Nazi doctors cited Holmes's opinion in *Buck v. Bell* as part of their defense. *Buck v. Bell* has never been officially overturned, even though the data indicates that the prime targets for eugenic sterilizations were poor Whites and poor people of color. Mexican American and Native American women were also targeted as recently as the 1960s.

A few paragraphs back, I referred to isms with specific characteristics common to some but not all of them. The characteristics are the following:

1. Is it represented by an organizational group identity?
2. Does it recruit and maintain a membership?
3. Does it collect funds from said membership?
4. Does it promote and define a philosophy of life?
5. Does it use its funds in the promotion of its philosophy of life by means of political advocacy?
6. Does it exert political pressure on both candidates for political office as well as upon elected officials to comply with its philosophy of life?
7. Does it contribute to political campaigns?
8. Does it endorse candidates sympathetic to its philosophy of life?
9. Does it lobby to have its philosophy of life promulgated through legislation?

Numbers 1–4 would not apply, for example, to sexism or to Neoplatonism, hedonism, or any number of current philosophies as so many of them have a "live and let live" characteristic that does not lend itself to organization as much as to self-application. But what if there is a school of thought or philosophy that does in fact have those first four characteristics? They could be the Kiwanis or Rotary Club as they are service organizations and not merely theoretical philosophies. The first four characteristics are shared by churches of all religious denominations as well, but we would not expect either the Kiwanis or the Presbyterians to engage in the activities delineated in 5–9.

In the United States, because of our history and the struggle for religious freedom that was from the outset of the founding of the New England colonies, there was a very clear sense of what it meant to have someone else's values and worldview imposed upon the masses. What was never considered is that the exact same dynamic of the imposition of one organization's beliefs could occur when the group or organization was not a religion at all but a philosophy of life or a nontheistic worldview. Thus, we have been cast in the position of straining a gnat and swallowing a camel by our narrowness of definition as it applies to the First Amendment that has in turn created a loophole and a grossly unlevel playing field as it were. Atheism can be represented by the organizations American Atheists or the Freedom from Religion Foundation to advance their political agendas without having to worry that the legal criteria of the First Amendment could ever be applied to their attempts at promoting legislation that reflects their worldview. Breitbart News can hide behind the protection of freedom of the press as it promotes white nationalism and populism that have had a direct influence on the policy positions that came from the White House. The American Humanist Association is free to "proselytize" its views onto government policy without raising any suspicion at all. The First Amendment does not apply to such groups merely because of a theistic versus nontheistic distinction. Groups that for all practical purposes function as a religion in membership, shared philosophy and generation of funds have an ocean-wide loophole to freely step through without any hinderance at all. They are free to impose their beliefs with the support of the government and furthermore have the government enact laws and federal guidelines according to their beliefs. These laws range from enacting nationalistic border policy to promotion of particular sex education policies.

Earlier in this chapter, I described how the fourth category includes special interest groups or lobbyists who are in fact surrogates for the first three categories. These entities promote their agendas with impunity and come from both the left and the right. Now before you dismiss this "fourth category" as completely absurd, please note that such machinations do have historical precedent.

Now organizations within the fourth category have had historical success at achieving their philosophical goals and imposing their worldview on the rest of the country as the Constitution itself was manipulated by evangelical Christians in their successful promotion of the Eighteenth Amendment. Even though official denominational sponsorship of the amendment would have been suspect, the temperance movement, an umbrella term used to include the Anti-Saloon League of America and the Women's Christian Temperance Union, among others, was able to mobilize Protestant churches to organize political entities and to raise the needed funds in creation of the political influence necessary for the passage of the Volstead Act. This is historical fact, and since we have not learned from the past, we make the same errors in the present.

I as a Catholic place no particular importance on the welfare of the secular state of Israel and in particular upon the city of Jerusalem. The new Jerusalem mentioned in the book of Revelation has little if anything to do with the secular state of Israel from my Catholic theological perspective. So how is it that evangelical Christians had so much influence on the Trump administration when it came to the issue of recognizing

Jerusalem as the capital of Israel? How is it that their theological perspective was pandered to by the changing of American policy, a policy by which loyal evangelicals show their appreciation at the ballot box?

How is it that popular sociopolitical opinions regarding sexual orientation and gender identity can successfully tilt legislative scales to their advantage without ever having to be challenged as a surrogate for humanism with its disdain for people with religious views? Where is the science? Where is the dialogue? Where is the process? All of a sudden, President Obama and Vice President Biden had an epiphany regarding the rights of those who practice homosexuality and then marriage between people of the same sex became the law of the land? Did I miss something? And what if I disagree? What if I missed the epiphany train?

In *Citizens United*, the Supreme Court's 2010 decision, corporations officially joined the ranks of other surrogate isms with emboldened means to influence the American political landscape within the fourth category that sidesteps current interpretation of the First Amendment. Though many major lobbying entities serve their own business interests, not all participate in engendering philosophical opinions from their well-heeled sources. Those that do would include Christians United for Israel and even the NRA that has a mind- numbing effect on its loyal minions and has become a religion for all practical purposes with the ironic consequence that the Constitution, and the distorted interpretation of the Second Amendment, has become its holy text. The Mercer Family Foundation might also be an entity for further scrutiny as it exists to further a sociophilosophical agenda through political means.

In addressing specific points of conflict, I would first address the religion in school issue. From my perspective, neither the Establishment Clause nor the Free Exercise Clause applied to this matter. No specific religious affiliation was being required from or infringed upon someone else's religious belief that I could see. The general concept of belief in a deity and the requirement of the state to profess belief in a deity was not the subject of concern for the framers of the Constitution yet because of our antagonistically based judicial system. Madeline Murray O'Hair was able to take a minority view and have it imposed on the rest of the nation without any dialogue at all. The real problems that were not addressed involved local mandatory prayer in school and/or reading of the Bible in school and ended up with the complete prohibition of religious practices in public schools. Imagine if every marital conflict sidestepped communication and attempts at resolution and went immediately to divorce court. You would arrive at a judicial decision but not necessarily a resolution to the underlying problems. Instead of addressing the tendency of local school districts imposing their version of official religion on captive students, all students were now prohibited from expressing their faith. We lack the creative means of arriving at consensus and a mutual appreciation of each other's concerns when we get stuck in the false dichotomy of judicial either/or. One side manipulated their will on the country, millions of Americans felt that their voice was irrelevant, and as a result, the country changed—not necessarily for the better.

Where the rubber meets the road is in the public schools that our children attend and in the workplace; in the former, we impart our common values, and in the latter, we either succeed or fail to realize those same values. But what happens when we have either lost sight of common values or come to the realization that we don't have too many common values left? Should a state-funded school sanction, teach, and impose practices on children that are in direct conflict with any child's upbringing? This ranges from forcing an agnostic student to participate in Bible readings to handing out condoms and promoting homosexuality as either inborn or abnormal. Should children in such a school be victimized and murdered because one entity promulgates that assault rifles are protected by the Second Amendment? Should the teaching of science be politicized and compromised by interests on the left or the right?

We as adults do not even have the skills to dialogue constructively on these issues of great moral import, so how can we impart what we lack to our children? What if instead children fleshed out the Free Exercise Clause without insisting that everyone had to believe identically to each other so that the idea of live and let live became foundational to appreciating what we do have in common? Mutual respect for others would outweigh all other considerations so that religious freedom would in fact be lived from the ground up and not legislated from the top down as most of these legislative efforts are concerned with imposing a worldview on others.

To wrap up this chapter, I would like to go back to my previous reference to Article Six and how it applies to the nomination process of Supreme Court justices. If both the Republicans and the Democrats use the issue of abortion and the position of potential candidates to the Supreme Court as a litmus test to even consider appointment to the Supreme Court, how is this not a direct violation of Article Six? How is this not then a required religious test?

TWELVE

THE EMPEROR IS BUTT NAKED: THE TRUMP PROBLEM, THE US PROBLEM

> One day, two rogues, calling themselves weavers,
> made their appearance. They gave out that they
> knew how to weave stuffs of the most beautiful
> colors and elaborate patterns, the clothes
> manufactured from which should have the
> wonderful property of remaining invisible to
> everyone who was unfit for the office he held, or
> who was extraordinarily simple in character.

"THE EMPEROR'S NEW CLOTHES"
(HANS CHRISTIAN ANDERSEN)

Premise and Perspective

The title of this chapter speaks for itself without further elucidation, yet at this point, it is necessary for my full disclosure on the subject of Donald Trump as I can make no claim to objectivity regarding my estimation of the man. Notice that I jump right into premise and perspective without any attempt to deceive myself with faux objective analysis or observations. First of all, I don't hate him and I don't wish him ill. The problem is that I don't trust him at all not to first serve himself and his image and his sense of legacy long before he would feign interest in serving the country. I wouldn't care if he masterfully supported every issue that I hold dear, which he doesn't. It would not change my assessment that Trump is all about Trump.

I would like to make a big *T*/little *t* distinction here as it applies not to truth but to trust in the area of politics and life in general. Though I have voted for both Republicans and Democrats in the past, I still consider myself an independent. As I critically examine individuals, such as Nancy Pelosi and Joe Biden, I as a Catholic have several issues with their version of Catholicism. I have small *t* trust issues with them as I do with most politicians in that even though I have no doubt that Pelosi did in fact pray for the president, standing on one's faith upbringing concerning prayer with one face and promoting what is clearly against the teachings of the church concerning abortion with another face does not help me to trust her. The Biden who supports the Hyde Amendment when it is politically expedient and then casts it aside when it no longer serves his political ambitions makes him one of a tidal wave of politicians for whom little *t* trust is broken within me on a regular basis. In life as in politics, little *t* trust is essential in building authentic relationships and in discerning that one is not casting one's pearls or one's votes before swine.

The distinction here with big *T* trust is seen in the trauma of dealing with an unfaithful spouse or in the eyes of a sexually abused child or in the struggle of African Americans to believe that justice can really exist for them in our justice system. As is plain for all to see, Trust is not on the same level as say not being able to trust that my goodies in the office refrigerator will go untouched throughout the day.

My discernment is woefully colored by the fact that I do not have Trust in Donald Trump at all. I see no truth in him so I need to discern where I stand and reflect upon what truth is when truthfulness is abandoned. I look to scripture for guidance.

First John 1:5–10 says, "Now this is the message that we have heard from him and proclaim to you: God is light, and in him there is no darkness at all."

If we say, "We have fellowship with him," while we continue to walk in darkness, we lie and do not act in truth.

But if we walk in the light as He is in the light, then we have fellowship with one another, and the blood of his Son Jesus cleanses us from all sin.

If we say, "We are without sin," we deceive ourselves, and the truth is not in us. If we acknowledge our sins, He is faithful and just and will forgive our sins and cleanse us from every wrongdoing.

If we say, "We have not sinned," we make Him a liar, and His word is not in us.

Ultimately, the issue is not about Donald Trump himself, for he is merely a symptom of the times. The fundamental question revolves around those who blindly defend him in an almost cultlike fashion and also around those who are so filled with hate and rage over him that they have lost themselves in their anger. In a way, both groups have sold their souls to their respective causes and have abandoned any notion or desire for discernment. They are both convinced that they are acting according to God's will without truly seeking God's will. From a nonspiritual perspective, each side is so biased in their sense of what is right and legal that they have abandoned any attempt to discern what is truth or wherein lies justice. There exist some preconditions among those who are inclined to find demagoguery appealing, and it doesn't make any difference if one considers oneself to be conservative or liberal. Calling oneself progressive seems a bit self-congratulatory to me, thank you.

Here are some basic principles in discerning about the message and the messenger:

1. Does the messenger engage in character assassination?
2. Does the messenger use divisive language?
3. Does the messenger spend more energy casting blame than in finding solutions?
4. Does the messenger create litmus tests to measure fidelity to ideology?
5. Is the messenger dismissive of criticism or does he or she welcome other perspectives?
6. Is the messenger honest and trustworthy?
7. Is the messenger arrogant or personify the leadership trait of humility?
8. Who is financing the message? Who holds the purse strings?
9. How consistent has the messenger been in matters of principle and ethics?
10. Is the messenger attempting to sow seeds of doubt and mistrust?
11. Does the messenger cite conspiracy theories as real evidence of anything?
12. Does the messenger value ideology over the real needs of real people in the name of those same people?

Identifying red flags in my unwillingness or indifference about discerning truth of any kind, particularly when it may lead to contradiction of a long-cherished belief or bias, is a major step toward humility. It isn't so much a matter of completely giving up one's attachment to core principles or religious beliefs as much as it is a matter of straining out those inconsistencies in myself that contradict my interpretation of these same said principles or religious beliefs. These are some possible red flags:

1. Am I attracted to or repulsed by character assassination of any kind for any reason?
2. Am I inclined to believe the most despicable rumor about somebody?
3. Do I ignore my own conscience in areas where my behavior contradicts my real core values but does not contradict my peer values?
4. Have I allowed my core values to become compromised or watered down by my lifestyle and political positions?
5. Do I tend to belittle those who disagree with me?
6. Am I drawn to divisiveness or to unity?
7. Do I value perceived personal rights over the common good and the rights of others?
8. Do I defend either my political party or my country, right or wrong?
9. Do I admire arrogance in leaders?
10. Do I prefer to remain ignorant on issues where my conscience tells me that I am in the wrong? This last one is my major hurdle.
11. Am I so crippled by a lack of trust that I am on the verge of giving up on the country altogether?

What I can't do is give in to one-dimensional conclusions by overlooking inconsistencies in thinking created by the gross assumption that one has to be on one side of the fence or the other. Allow me to share how my very real "perspective"—perspective in every sense of the word—does not bind one from seeing beyond the linear backbiting because the big picture is more accurate and more honest than my limited perspective.

As a social conservative, I am deeply concerned about the government vis a vis the public schools influencing the lives of young people by handing out condoms as part of sex education. It supports a single philosophy of sexuality by its sanctioning the use of condoms and is in fact, from both my life perspective and my memories of what it was like to be an adolescent male, giving a green light to premarital sex. I am not asking you to agree with me, but please indulge me a little further. I also believe that LGBTQ "reality" becoming the norm in public schools circumvents the rights of parents and children who do not agree. I believe that a green light is being given to sexual ambiguity and experimentation. I believe that both of these examples have a harmful effect on children and will have negative consequences as a direct result of state approval and the contradiction of their upbringing, in the process of becoming responsible adults.

Now with all that said, whether you agree with me or not, what I don't understand is that a large swath of the population fully agrees with my aforementioned comments about oppressive school policies and the harmful effects on children while still approving of and blindly supporting the name-calling and bullying of Donald Trump. How do they not see that approval and support of this kind of behavior will have long-lasting effects on American children? How can they not see that a significant green light is being given to arrogance, racism, and narcissistic behavior? How can they not see that a green light is being given to outright lies and slander? Even if you believe that voting for Trump was a single-issue vote, how can you buy the snake oil of hatred and division he has sown in this country?

Dealing directly with the issue of abortion, the bottom line is that I don't trust Donald Trump at all as he manipulates the truth with a casual disregard and has figured out that he could mobilize more votes by claiming to be pro-life than by going back to his previous position of being pro-choice. Yes, he will offer to sell people the Brooklyn Bridge and have said bridge plastered with American flags, gun rights slogans, and pro-life posters and the line of people lining up to buy it will reach to the horizon. This cult of personality is really not all that different from the appeal of Bernie Sanders. Trump has the "swamp," and Bernie has the "1 percent," both of which take the quixotic place of windmills for those who feel disenfranchised and want an alternative to politics as usual.

The bottom line for me is that I try to the best of my ability to reflect the whole message of what I believe pro-life means. In spite of the fact that Trump's political messaging and Supreme Court nominations seem to reflect a strong antiabortion position, the myopia of this position excludes every other dimension of what pro-life encompasses. I also operate from a foundational moral principle that the ends never justify the means. I would need a frontal lobotomy and perhaps the loss of my soul before I could ever support Trump. As I stated in another chapter, the issue of abortion is fundamentally a spiritual one to me and not a political one as life is devalued at every level of our society. It is almost as if one could naively believe that passage of the Civil Rights Act of 1964 automatically eliminated racism. Before the 2016 Presidential campaign, I naively believed that we had come a long way in the area of race relations, but I was dead wrong as white supremacists, neo-Nazis, and KKK members have all crawled out from under their rocks and were given safe haven under the Trump administration.

Now with all this said, I have dear friends and people I care for deeply who voted for Trump. Once again, I don't get it, but my getting it is not the issue. What is really at stake is my willingness and my ability to embrace the messiness of diversity, the inefficiency of democracy, and the challenge of pluralism. Each individual needs to discern without coercion as to how to think and believe and vote accordingly. I would say, "Run. Don't walk away from preachers who would dare tell you how to vote. They are dangerous not only to their congregations by shamelessly stepping way over the line between church and state but mostly because they show a complete disregard for the sacredness of the individual conscience and the process of discernment."

I don't believe that Trump is particularly eloquent or cogent in either oratorical delivery or tweet, but since the bar of expectations had been lowered accordingly, I at least attempted to listen to what he was trying to communicate. Pretty much all my friends and acquaintances who are definite "haters" didn't dare risk giving Trump the benefit of the doubt in anything he said or did. They found evil intent in everything that Trump attempted. As I write these lines, it is mid-March 2020 and the COVID-19 pandemic is getting a full head of steam here in the United States and economic fears are being realized every day in the stock market and mostly in the lives of millions of people who are finding themselves without employment. People are dying every day and the worst is yet to come, so I fail to see how expending one ounce of energy criticizing Trump and how he should have handled this crisis has any value at all, but the haters rail on anyway. A time will come when such evaluation will be of value, but it isn't at the present. To bring balance to this social climate that breeds toilet paper hoarding, it is encouraging that individuals, local leaders, and governors have taken up the slack in how to respond, because living in a world of "should'ves" and finger-pointing accomplishes nothing positive and is not concerned with real-time solutions.

The same complete blindness that allows some to see nothing wrong in Donald Trump also allows some to see nothing redeemable in Donald Trump. This further illustrates how he is merely a symptom of our national dysfunction. The Trump problem is no greater than the "us" problem in that we bear responsibility for how divided we have become as a nation and also for how far we are willing to let our country break apart at the seams. Living in a time of crisis may give us an opportunity to see if we are more concerned with blame and political outcomes or dedicated to pulling together to find common solutions. The medical caretakers who have put their own lives on the front lines for us probably represent a broad spectrum of political opinion and affiliation, and they deserve every resource we can provide them devoid of blame and excuses. Extreme common task orientation has a way of dissipating ideological wisps of smoke.

My hope is to reveal a sense of my moral and ethical process in how I have determined that I could never support Donald Trump.

> How good God is to the upright,
> to those who are pure of heart!
>
> But, as for me, my feet had almost stumbled;
> my steps had nearly slipped,
>
> Because I was envious of the arrogant
> when I saw the prosperity of the wicked.

For they suffer no pain;
their bodies are healthy and sleek.

They are free of the burdens of life;
they are not afflicted like others.

Thus pride adorns them as a necklace;
violence clothes them as a robe.

Out of such blindness comes sin;
evil thoughts flood their hearts.

They scoff and spout their malice;
from on high they utter threats.

They set their mouths against the heavens,
their tongues roam the earth.

So my people turn to them
and drink deeply of their words. (Psalm 73:1–
10 NAB)

THIRTEEN

THE MILLSTONE AND THE TRAP: AN EPISTLE TO CHRISTIANS

Whoever causes one of these little ones who believe
in me to sin, it would be better for him to have a great
millstone hung around his neck and to be drowned
in the depths of the sea. Woe to the world because
of things that cause sin! Such things must come,
but woe to the one through whom they come!

MATTHEW 18:6–7

The little ones in this quote from the gospel of Matthew can
be applied to children, young people, or new converts—those
generally young in the faith. I would apply it even more broadly
in our day and age to span from millennials through Gen Z, both
Christians and everyone else. The verb *skandalisey*, translated
as "causes one to sin," applies to the act of causing someone to
stumble. The word *escandalon* in Greek is most literally the stick
or triggering mechanism of a trap that causes a person to stumble
and fall into a pit of some kind. Think of setting someone up or

more literally tripping someone up through one's bad example or lack of awareness, resulting in discouragement or a loss of faith and return to sin.

True discernment always has a social dynamic and awareness so that it does not become some kind of false asceticism where navel gazing and Bible thumping leave little concern for the anawim and the rest of God's people broken down by the cruelties of life—those crushed in spirit. Essentially, seeking God's will is revealed in serving the needs of others and leads to the fulfillment of what is sought, which is ultimately manifested in serving the needs of others. In short, it is walking the walk. With that said, I would propose that hypocrisy is the escandalon by which the Christian churches drive people away by the millions as the gospel message gets so watered down—so lukewarm and twisted—that people are repulsed from so-called Christians who seem not to know the difference between right and wrong, just and unjust, and good and evil.

There are so many cultural, theological, and historical reasons why some Christian churches can be fixated upon material prosperity or Jesus being one's "personal" Savior or attaining salvation by uttering a formula for a guarantee of salvation without any further accountability. Although these beliefs form foundational differences in how some Christians define their reality—think of premise—there is nothing to be gained by rehashing old doctrinal arguments. Instead, I would like to focus on real-life responses to real-life moral issues and the positions and politics and lifestyles of "Christians."

In eventually transitioning from the micro to the macro, it is best to look at the simplest examples in life that provide opportunities for common experiences and common frustrations as we put up with our "neighbor" with varying degrees of success. What better common experience to examine than our automotive habits? Since we value our cars so much and we spend so much time driving, we have so many opportunities to set each other off, from small infractions to downright dangerous driving.

Before we call to mind the infractions that annoy us the most, let's look at how our self-centered universe already skews our driving perceptions. Have you ever noticed how when you are trying to merge into two-way traffic from a stopped position it feels like traffic from both directions is teaming up to thwart your efforts to merge? Have you ever noticed that some people merge right up the block from you to personally keep you from merging? And why do people intentionally speed up or slow down when you are trying to merge? Of course, all these observations are nonsensical when reading about them, but when these feelings are experienced in real time, we don't process logically, much less objectively, so the idea that the whole universe revolves around me and my transportation needs is not that far-fetched when in the moment. My moral development is at the level of an infant or toddler at these times where my perceived needs outweigh all other considerations.

When someone flips me off on the road, is my first response "What is their problem?" Or is it "What did I just do?" How unaware am I of how my less than perfect driving affects others, and do I even care? This experience is exemplary of the self-absorbed moral compass of an adolescent. Try explaining to a teenager what consideration means.

Now here is a discernment exercise in conscience and self-awareness, baby steps in the realm of driving that can be applied to more complex moral discernment.

1. Make a list of every example of lousy driving you have experienced from other drivers with special emphasis on

the ones where you have a strong emotional response. Pay particular attention to remembering what your adrenaline level felt like in collisions or near-miss collisions.

2. Make a list of your most common examples of poor driving.

If you are like most people, your first list is much longer than your second list. This may or may not be accurate, but it is not accuracy that we are after as much as it is a sense of disposition while getting behind the wheel of your vehicle. It is not my intention to sound condescending or disrespectful to the reader but to illustrate that it is in our most basic and common experiences that we get the most accurate measure of our moral maturity, if you will. An experience we share in common is the road construction merge where signs of the impending merge are displayed three miles before the merge takes place. What do you do? Are you *that* person? Now think of what a great example *that* person is setting, zooming past you on the right in the emergency lane just to get beyond more cars, especially when they have some church decal or bumper sticker. It's a running joke in a men's fellowship I belong to how there is nothing like getting cut off by someone with a (<u>fill in the blank</u>) religious sticker on their vehicle.

Perhaps the way we drive is the most accurate and most honest test of who we are and what we bear in our hearts. Have you ever noticed that sometimes the drivers who speed in school zones are in fact parents dropping off their own children, the very same children the school zones are supposed to protect? Do I graciously allow people to merge, or do I pull a power play? Am I aware of the road conditions, the traffic, and my surroundings, or do I text when I drive? The sins of omission in driving involve my lack of awareness of the needs of others while I serve my own interests behind the wheel of my universe, my needs, my reality. The most obvious practitioners of this myopia range from the extremes of those who never use a turn signal or habitually roll stops to the drunk and in these days stoned drivers with the result being nearly ten thousand traffic fatalities a year.

Even though all analogies are not quite perfect, it is safe to assume that these driving extremes cut across all political ideologies and range from atheistic humanists to religious fundamentalists of all stripes. No group has a monopoly on either self-centered or altruistic adherents. The comparisons I would like to make between our individual and collective driving habits and our individual and collective moral tendencies will hopefully become more obvious, particularly within the context of how good or bad an example I am, in driving as well as in living.

So let's look at some possible categories.

1. On one extreme, we have the drivers of the *law* who insist on driving in the passing lane at exactly the speed limit so as to say, "You shall drive in my image," to fellow drivers. Their parallel would be those moralists who know how everyone else should live under all circumstances. Such self-righteous behavior is not limited to the left or the right as they know what's best for everyone else.

2. The next category might be where most of us fit into: the "I observe most of the laws most of the time" category. I know what is expected, but I speed if I think I can get away with it. I feel justified by the fact that I have so few traffic citations, which really means I only get caught .005 percent of the time. This person in a moral sense is more concerned with getting caught and the

impending consequences. They adhere to a social moral ethic as convenience allows and are generally observant of guidelines but are well versed in rationalizations so as to not transition into a greater love response for others.

3. Another category would include the inconsiderate driver who rarely uses their turn signal and might even cut across four lanes of traffic to force an exit. This driver might also be one who always drives in the right lane on the freeway out of fear or anxiety, which creates more merges than necessary for the drivers trying to exit and for the drivers trying to enter the freeway. Their go-to justification is that it is not against the law to drive this way as long as there isn't an accident, completely unaware of how everybody else has to brake or swerve or compensate somehow because of their inconsiderate driving choices. Either example is reminiscent of people whose lifestyle decisions exist with a complete lack of awareness of how that very same lifestyle negatively impacts other people. This could be either affected ignorance or just not having the moral tools to even have a clue. They choose not to look behind the reason for morals or ethical behavior so they don't have to ever make real lifestyle changes as part of spiritual growth. They also look to the support of like-minded people who are content in not going beyond their moral rut. They probably sit in pew thirteen on the right side every week.

4. This fourth category refers to completely self-serving drivers. They truly believe that the rules don't apply to them. We have all experienced tailgaters, racers, weavers, phone/text junkies, drunks, etc. Their ability to justify and rationalize is only equaled by their complete disregard for the welfare of other drivers.

Even though a large percentage of these individuals are adolescents, not all of them are, and they are represented across demographics. The real-life parallels in moral characteristics are reflected in those with a glorified sense of individual freedom as the highest of moral virtues. They are represented from antifa-styled anarchists all the way to Tea Party diehards who share the same battle cry of all self-absorbed adolescents. "You aren't the boss of *me!*" What is essential to understand here in this imperfect analogy is that the implication is not that those in this moral category break the law and are terrible people as much as what I referred to before about the drivers. "It is not accuracy that we are after as much as it is a sense of disposition while getting behind the wheel of your vehicle." I would maintain that the common disposition that links these drivers and the moral self-servers is manifested in a sense of entitlement and superiority, even moral superiority. Their station in life allows for it. Their place in the church, or in high places of government for that matter, makes it acceptable. How can racism be immoral if I belong to the superior race? How can sexism be immoral if women would just accept their place? How can xenophobic immigration laws be immoral if I have a greater right to justice and dignity than foreigners do? How is it immoral to hate faggots when God hates them too? If Church-attending, Bible-school-teaching, tithing Christians believe any of that nonsense, then they shouldn't look so shocked when the "nones," those people who do not identify with any church tradition at all, make up over 23 percent of the US population.

A last category of driver is not on the one-dimensional line as the others are. It is as if they drive according to level 3 of Kohlberg's Stages of Moral Development. They look at the responsibility and privilege to drive as a social contract for the common good and even at times simply as a matter of personal integrity without concern for how it is perceived by others. I have a dear friend who lost two daughters as a consequence of drunk driving in two separate accidents. Imagine on his journey of healing and forgiveness how he views his own driving responsibilities and how this awareness impacts on who he is as a person. Incidentally, he was a presenter for MADD and for years addressed several hundred DWI/DUI offenders to share his story. The transition from established mindsets to compassion and relationship is the challenge for all who are truly devoted to the process of discernment and the movement of the Holy Spirit in their lives.

So you don't think that I am out to pick on evangelicals, my own faith family has failed miserably time and time again in coming to grips with the real consequences and culpability of the sexual abuse scandal. Notice the use of the word *scandal* and how differently we understand it from its original meaning. Aside from the unknown suicide attempts, both successful and unsuccessful, aside from those young victims who without the benefit of psychological help went on to become predators, which then led to the creation of more victims, aside from the years of suffering that transitioned emotionally crippled children into emotionally crippled adults, there exist consequences that the hierarchy of the church seems to be oblivious to. The sins of the predatory priests pale in comparison to the sins of the hierarchical enablers who laterally shifted these men from one flock of unsuspecting children to another to another. The trust of these children was abused. The trust of their families and parish communities was broken. Whatever moral authority the Church presumed to have was sacrificed at the altar of arrogance and secrecy.

Aside from all the very real aforementioned suffering, the collateral effect of this sin is the steady decline in church attendance with a 3 percent decrease among US Catholics in the past four years. One statistical breakdown I read a few years ago had Catholicism as the leading denomination in the country in terms of attendance, but what floored me was that if you totaled the number of ex-Catholics who are nones, they would make up the second largest group before any other denomination. The lateral consequences of causing whole generations to stumble, doubt, and leave will require massive quantities of massive millstones for the unrepentant guilty.

Not unlike the politics of the church, the politics of governance and representation also demonstrate the culpability of not only the perpetrators but of the enablers as well. This applies most concretely to Bill Clinton's thinking that he could get away with it as well as to Donald Trump's ability to actually get away with it. What is even more damning are the millions of evangelical "Christians" and conservative, single-issue Catholics who have given Trump a pass by ensuring that he continues to get away with it. Even the pagan "fake news" agencies knew that they could not ignore the allegations leveled against Matt Lauer, Charlie Rose, Glenn Thrush, Matt Zimmerman, Michael Oreskes, and Mark Halperin among others, and their dismissals came with only allegations, though some allegations were ignored for years. Brian Williams lost his top anchor position with NBC news for taking liberties with the truth. Even if concern for broadcast revenues and the fear of negative publicity were the main motivators for responding quickly in the current political climate, the integrity of various news agencies was also at stake in a medium where trust has always been a cornerstone. Conversely, as a result of the now infamous *Access Hollywood* conversation between Billy Bush and Donald Trump, Billy Bush was fired by NBC for being a cooperative listener to vulgarity and Trump was elected president of the United States. Williams exaggerated and enhanced his story and Trump misleads and downright lies as a matter of course but still comes up smelling like a rose to his evangelical supporters.

In a nutshell, young people from a myriad of backgrounds witnessed a president who gave tacit approval and a green light to white supremacists, who fanned the flames of xenophobic racism with the caging of children removed from their families and the divisive talk of building a wall, who has been accused by at least seventeen women of inappropriate sexual advances and beyond, who bullies and belittles those who disagree with him, and lastly, who seemed more concerned with how the economic effects of the COVID-19 pandemic reflected on him politically than for the people who were at risk and who were suffering. More importantly, these same young people have witnessed preachers and pastors throw in their lot with this man, with their congregations following without question and without any challenge of conscience. Yet here are more passive forms of enablement to be examined.

Going back to driving analogies, could you imagine a road rage situation where two people in conflict actually pulled off to the side of the road, got out of their vehicles, and then started wailing on each other? It does happen, but let's take the analogy one step further. Imagine that other drivers started pulling off to the side of the road, took sides, and also started throwing blows so that the initial brawl turned into a violent battle with every participant feeling justified in their public display of hatred. As absurd as that sounds, it plays out every day online among faith-filled people across the political spectrum with more rationalized self-righteousness than can be truly understood as it is pure online rage and is just as irrational as the aforementioned violent mob. Feeling goaded into a response and becoming an active participant in the hatred goes way beyond enabling negative behavior. Enabling this everyday phenomenon is more in the realm of a sin of omission. Failing to stand up against hatred from all sides online and remaining silent is enablement in itself. If a "friend" on Facebook has gone way off the deep end as indicated by slander, obscenity-laced rants, and the language of hatred, are you going to let that friend go unchallenged? Even if you are sympathetic to your friend's viewpoints, are you going to remain silent and avoid at all costs the risks entailed in brotherly or sisterly correction? Causing others to stumble by means of unchecked anger and hatred online is bad enough. Think back on the clerical child molesters. Remaining silent and not acting when one sees the traps, the danger, and the consequences now becomes the greater sin. Think back on the hierarchical protectors of the faith. These words from Frederick Nietzsche could easily come from any one of the "nones": "I might believe in the Redeemer if his followers looked more redeemed."

This final indictment pertains to the cabal of evangelical snake handlers who embedded themselves and their influence in the White House and who preach a gospel of defiance by gathering their flocks during a pandemic as a sign of faith when in fact they are only tempting fate by disobeying the law of love. The whole world watched as the president of the United States kowtowed to this lot by continuously downplaying the significance of what was at the time an epidemic. My heart goes out to the members of those misguided churches that they and their loved ones do not suffer from what they are bringing on themselves by mistaking pride for faith. I pray that those in the surrounding communities are protected from COVID-19 as a result of the complete absence of charity brought about by those who would test God. I pray that those who are weak in faith may not stumble as a result of the callous disregard for human life that these "Christians" displayed for all to see. I pray that the vast majority of Christians may bear a harvest of good fruit to reveal the mercy of God as we care for those in need in this time of crises so that the rotten fruit of false prophets may not be piled so high as to keep people from the love of Christ. I pray for people of all faiths and for those who express no need of faith that we may be drawn to serve and to love and to become the people we were created to be in the unity of the Creator.

At some point, the common need so far outweighs the rhetorical/ideological differences that we must allow ourselves to become overwhelmed with the light of discernment that overcomes and dispels all the darkness and division. We need each other. Even before we can discern, we must relearn how to trust again. I must learn how to trust again.

POSTSCRIPT JULY 30, 2020

George Floyd. Breonna Taylor. Ahmaud Arbery.
COVID-19 Deaths to Date: (US) 153,769; (Global) 668,801

Impressions and Snippets

I naively believed that provided with sincerity and clarity, most people would reconsider their positions and as a result would consider listening to those who see differently and think differently from themselves. These are the people I hoped would use this book to further greater appreciation and respect for others. As the vitriol online has reached a fever pitch in 2020 during an election year, I have modified my expectations and now hope that maybe just "people of good will" might use some of the ideas offered to find purpose and discernment in their relationships with others. As such, I have come to the following conclusions:

> The hardened heart is not only impervious to science, to reason, and to facts but also resists the action of the Holy Spirit to turn away from self-centeredness and pride. The hardened heart of the sinner has a greater chance of being softened through mercy and compassion than does the hardened heart of the follower of religious precepts who sees no need to repent.

I have been sitting on the fence too long concerning climate change. All the skeptics of the pandemic, mask wearing, and social distancing who promote pseudoscience misinformation have helped me see more clearly. If they can't accept science when fellow citizens are dying by the hundreds of thousands, waiting for them to get on board in addressing climate change is a fool's errand. Thanks for clearing that up for me.

Does your faith inform your politics, or does your politics utilize your faith for justification?

The left turns a blind eye to the violence of looting, vandalism, and tearing down statues as it worships the golden calf of anger and rationalized hatred where innocent people suffer. The right turns a blind eye to institutional violence that permits and promotes injustice in policing, banking, medical care, and educational opportunities as it worships Baal in the form of watered-down Christianity where, again, innocent people suffer. Both sides also worship Mammon in either the hoarding of wealth or the coveting of wealth to the diminishment of human dignity.

> Therefore, once for all this short command is
> given to you: "Love and do what you will." If
> you keep silent, keep silent by love: if you speak,
> speak by love; if you correct, correct by love; if
> you pardon, pardon by love; let love be rooted
> in you, and from the root nothing but good can
> grow. (St. Augustine of Hippo)

If you have really sought to discern the most loving response in the formation of your conscience and you follow Augustine's teaching, then always vote your conscience, but do not judge others as they vote theirs.

Discernment casts light onto darkness, not only in my own soul but also upon the world in times of confusion and hopelessness. It is always rooted in humility.

Skepticism creates darkness and doubt and feeds on fear and cynicism. It creates its own "truth" so as to lead others into despair and anger. It is built on self-righteousness and "moral" principles that defy discernment and the formation of conscience. It is always rooted in pride.

The beginning of compassion is an appreciation for the mercy that has been given me.

The beginning of unity is in the appreciation for God's infinite diversity.

The beginning of wisdom is in putting your shopping cart away and in poop-scooping after your dog. All other wisdom will follow.